T0215335

Computer Vision with Maker Tech

Detecting People With a Raspberry Pi, a Thermal Camera, and Machine Learning

Fabio Manganiello

Apress®

Computer Vision with Maker Tech: Detecting People With a Raspberry Pi, a Thermal Camera, and Machine Learning

Fabio Manganiello
Amsterdam, The Netherlands

ISBN-13 (pbk): 978-1-4842-6820-9
https://doi.org/10.1007/978-1-4842-6821-6

ISBN-13 (electronic): 978-1-4842-6821-6

Managing Director, Apress Media LLC: Welmoed Spahr
Acquisitions Editor: Aaron Black
Development Editor: James Markham
Coordinating Editor: Jessica Vakili

Distributed to the book trade worldwide by Springer Science+Business Media New York, 1 NY Plazar, New York, NY 10014. Phone 1-800-SPRINGER, fax (201) 348-4505, e-mail orders-ny@springer-sbm.com, or visit www.springeronline.com. Apress Media, LLC is a California LLC and the sole member (owner) is Springer Science + Business Media Finance Inc (SSBM Finance Inc). SSBM Finance Inc is a **Delaware** corporation.

For information on translations, please e-mail booktranslations@springernature.com; for reprint, paperback, or audio rights, please e-mail bookpermissions@springernature.com.

Apress titles may be purchased in bulk for academic, corporate, or promotional use. eBook versions and licenses are also available for most titles. For more information, reference our Print and eBook Bulk Sales web page at http://www.apress.com/bulk-sales.

Any source code or other supplementary material referenced by the author in this book is available to readers on GitHub via the book's product page, located at www.apress.com/978-1-4842-6820-9. For more detailed information, please visit http://www.apress.com/source-code.

Printed on acid-free paper

Table of Contents

About the Author

Fabio Manganiello has more than 15 years of experience in software engineering, many of these spent working on machine learning and distributed systems. In his career he has worked, among others, on natural language processing, an early voice assistant (Voxifera) developed back in 2008, and machine learning applied to intrusion detection systems, using both supervised and unsupervised learning; and he has developed and released several libraries to make models' design and training easier, from back-propagation neural networks (Neuralpp) to self-organizing maps (fsom), to dataset clustering. He has contributed to the design of machine learning models for anomaly detection and image similarity in his career as a tech lead in Booking. com. In the recent years, he has combined his passion for machine learning with IoT and distributed systems. From self-driving robots to people detection, to anomaly detection, to weather forecasting, he likes to combine the flexibility and affordability of tools such as Raspberry Pi, Arduino, ESP8266, and cheap sensors with the power of machine learning models. He's an active IEEE member and open source enthusiast and has contributed to around 100 open source projects over the years. He is the creator and main contributor of Platypush, an all-purpose platform for automation that aims to connect any device to any service, and also provides TensorFlow and OpenCV integrations for machine learning.

About the Technical Reviewer

Vishwesh Ravi Shrimali graduated from BITS Pilani, where he studied mechanical engineering, in 2018. Since then, he has worked with Big Vision LLC on deep learning and computer vision and was involved in creating official OpenCV AI courses. Currently, he is working at Mercedes-Benz Research and Development India Pvt. Ltd. He has a keen interest in programming and AI and has applied that interest in mechanical engineering projects. He has also written multiple blogs on OpenCV and deep learning on Learn OpenCV, a leading blog on computer vision. He has also coauthored *Machine Learning for OpenCV 4* (second edition) by Packt. When he is not writing blogs or working on projects, he likes to go on long walks or play his acoustic guitar.

Introduction

The field of machine learning has gone through a massive growth in the last few years, thanks to increased computing power, increased funding, and better frameworks that make it easier to build and train classifiers. Machine learning, however, is still considered as a tool for IT giants with plenty of resources, data, and computing power. While it is true that models get better when they can be trained with more data points, and computing power surely plays a role in the ability to train complex models, in this book we'll see that it's already possible to build models trained on data points gathered from a smart home environment (like temperature, humidity, presence, or camera images), and you can already use those models to make your home "smarter." Such models can be used for predictions even on a Raspberry Pi or similar hardware.

After reading this book, you will

- Know the formal foundations of the main machine learning techniques

- Know how to estimate how accurate a classifier is in making predictions and what to tweak in order to improve its performance

- Know how to cleanse and preprocess your data points to maximize the performance of your models

- Be able to build machine learning models using TensorFlow and the standard Python stack for data analysis (numpy, matplotlib, pandas)

- Be able to set up a Raspberry Pi with a simple network of sensors, cameras, or other data sources that can be used to generate data points fed to simple machine learning models, make predictions on those data points, and easily create, train, and deploy models through web services

Chapters at a Glance

Chapter 1 will go through the theoretical foundations of machine learning. It will cover the most popular approaches to machine learning, the difference between supervised and unsupervised learning, and take a deep dive into regression algorithms (the foundation block for most of today's supervised learning). It will also cover the most popular strategies to visualize, evaluate, and tweak the performance of a model.

Chapter 2 will take a deep dive into neural networks, how they operate and "learn," and how they use computer vision. It will also cover convolutional neural networks (CNNs), a popular architecture used in most of today's computer vision classification models.

Chapter 3 will provide an overview of the most common tools used by makers in IoT today with a particular focus on the Raspberry Pi. We'll see how to use one of these devices to collect, send, and store data points that can be used to train machine learning models, and to train a simple model to detect the presence of people in a room using a cheap camera, and how to use it to make predictions within a home automation flow— for example, turn the lights on/off when presence is detected or send a notification when presence is detected but we are not home. The chapter will also provide an introduction to some strategies for semi-supervised learning and show how to wrap a web service around TensorFlow to programmatically create, train, and manage models.

CHAPTER 1

Introduction to Machine Learning

Machine learning is defined as the set of techniques to perform through a machine a task it wasn't explicitly programmed for. It is sometimes seen as a subset of *dynamic programming*. If you have some prior experience with traditional programming, you'll know that building a piece of software involves explicitly providing a machine with an unambiguous set of instructions to be executed sequentially or in parallel in order to perform a certain task. This works quite well if the purpose of your software is to calculate the commission on a purchase, or display a dashboard to the user, or read and write data to an attached device. These types of problems usually involve a finite number of well-defined steps in order to perform their task. However, what if the task of your software is to recognize whether a picture contains a cat? Even if you build a software that is able to correctly identify the shape of a cat on a few specific sample pictures (e.g., by checking whether some specific pixels present in your sample pictures are in place), that software will probably fail at performing its task if you provide it with different pictures of cats—or even slightly edited versions of your own sample images. And what if you have to build a software to detect spam? Sure, you can probably still do it with traditional programming—you can, for instance, build a huge list of words or phrases often found in spam emails—but if your software is provided with words similar to those on your list but that are not present on your list, then it will probably fail its task.

© Fabio Manganiello 2021
F. Manganiello, *Computer Vision with Maker Tech*,
https://doi.org/10.1007/978-1-4842-6821-6_1

The latter category includes tasks that traditionally humans have been considered better at performing than machines: a machine is million times faster than a human at executing a finite sequence of steps and even solving advanced math problems, but it'll shamefully fail (at least with traditional programming) at telling whether a certain picture depicts a cat or a traffic light. Human brains are usually better than machines in these tasks because they have been exposed for several years to many examples and sense-based *experiences*. We can tell within a fraction of a second whether a picture contains a cat even without having full experience about all the possible breeds and their characteristics and all of their possible poses. That's because we've probably seen other cats before, and we can quickly perform a process of mental *classification* that labels the subject of a picture as something that we have already seen in the past. In other words, our brains have been *trained*, or *wired*, over the years to become very good at recognizing *patterns* in a fuzzy world, rather than quickly performing a finite sequence of complex but deterministic tasks in a virtual world.

Machine learning is the set of techniques that tries to mimic the way our brains perform tasks—by trial and error until we can infer patterns out of the acquired experience, rather than by an explicit declaration of steps.

It's worth providing a quick disambiguation between *machine learning* and *artificial intelligence* (AI). Although the two terms are often used as synonyms today, machine learning is a set of techniques where a machine can be instructed to solve problems it wasn't specifically programmed for through exposure to (usually many) examples. Artificial intelligence is a wider classification that includes any machine or algorithm good at performing tasks usually humans are better at—or, according to some, tasks that display some form of human-like intelligence. The actual definition of AI is actually quite blurry—some may argue whether being able to detect an object in a picture or the shortest path between two cities is really a form of "intelligence"—and machine learning may be just one possible tool for achieving it (expert systems, for example, were quite popular in the early 2000s). Therefore, through this book I'll usually talk about the tool (machine learning algorithms) rather than the philosophical goal (artificial intelligence) that such algorithms may be supposed to achieve.

Before we dive further into the nuts and bolts of machine learning, it's probably worth providing a bit of context and history to understand how the discipline has evolved over the years and where we are now.

1.1 History

Although machine learning has gone through a very sharp rise in popularity over the past decade, it's been around probably as long as digital computers have been around. The dream of building a machine that could mimic human behavior and features with all of their nuances is even older than computer science itself. However, the discipline went through a series of ups and downs over the second half of the past century before experiencing today's explosion.

Today's most popular machine learning techniques leverage a concept first theorized in 1949 by Donald Hebb [1]. In his book *The Organization of Behavior*, he first theorized that neurons in a human brain work by either strengthening or weakening their mutual connections in response to stimuli from the outer environment. Hebb wrote, "When one cell repeatedly assists in firing another, the axon of the first cell develops synaptic knobs (or enlarges them if they already exist) in contact with the soma of the second cell." Such a model (fire together, wire together) inspired research into how to build an artificial neuron that could communicate with other neurons by dynamically adjusting the *weight* of its links to them (*synapses*) in response to the experience it gathers. This concept is the theoretical foundation behind modern-day neural networks.

One year later, in 1950, the famous British mathematician (and father of computer science) Alan Turing came with what is probably the first known definition of artificial intelligence. He proposed an experiment where a human was asked to have a conversation with "someone/something" hidden behind a screen. If by the end of the conversation the subject couldn't tell whether he/she had talked to a human or a machine, then the machine would have passed the "artificial intelligence" test. Such a test is today famously known as *Turing test*.

In 1951, Christopher Strachey wrote a program that could play checkers, and Dietrich Prinz, one that could play chess. Later improvements during the 1950s led to the development of programs that could effectively challenge an amateur player. Such early developments led to games being often used as a standard benchmark for measuring the progress of machine learning—up to the day when IBM's Deep Blue beat Kasparov at chess and AlphaGo beat Lee Sedol at Go.

In the meantime, the advent of digital computers in the mid-1950s led a wave of optimism in what became known as the *symbolic AI*. A few researchers recognized that a machine that could manipulate numbers could also manipulate symbols, and if symbols were the foundation of human thought, then it would have been possible to design thinking machines. In 1955, Allen Newell and the future Nobel laureate Herbert A. Simon created the *Logic Theorist*, a program that could prove mathematical theorems through inference given a set of logic axioms. It managed to prove 38 of the first 52 theorems of Bertrand Russell's *Principia Mathematica*.

Such theoretical background led to early enthusiasm among researchers. It caused a boost of optimism that culminated in a workshop held in 1956 at Dartmouth College [2], where some academics predicted that machines as intelligent as humans would have been available within one generation and were provided with millions of dollars to make the vision come true. This conference is today considered as the foundation of *artificial intelligence* as a discipline.

In 1957, Frank Rosenblatt designed the *perceptron*. He applied Hebb's neural model to design a machine that could perform image recognition. The software was originally designed for the IBM 704 and installed on a custom-built machine called the *Mark 1 perceptron*. Its main goal was to recognize features from pictures—facial features in particular. A perceptron functionally acts like a single neuron that can *learn* (i.e., adjust its synaptic weights) from provided examples and make predictions or guesses on examples it had never seen before. The mathematical procedure at the basis of the perceptron (*logistic regression*) is the building block of neural networks, and we'll cover it later in this chapter.

Despite the direction was definitely a good one to go, the network itself was relatively simple, and the hardware in 1957 definitely couldn't allow the marvels possible with today's machines. Whenever you wonder whether a Raspberry Pi is the right choice for running machine learning models, keep in mind that you're handling a machine almost a million times more powerful than the one used by Frank Rosenblatt to train the first model that could recognize a face [4, 5].

The disappointment after the perceptron experiment led to a drop of interest in the field of machine learning as we know it today (which only rose again during the late 1990s, when improved hardware started to show the potential of the theory), while more focus was put on other branches of artificial intelligence. The 1960s and 1970s saw in particular a rise in *reasoning as search*, an approach where the problem of finding a particular solution was basically translated as a problem of searching for paths in connected graphs that represented the available knowledge. Finding how "close" the meanings of two words were became a problem of finding the shortest path between the two associated nodes within a semantic graph. Finding the best move in a game of chess became a problem of finding the path with *minimum cost* or *maximum profit* in the graph of all the possible scenarios. Proving whether a theorem was true or false became a problem of building a *decision tree* out of its propositions plus the relevant axioms and finding a path that could lead either to a true or false statement. The progress in these areas led to impressive early achievements, such as ELIZA, today considered as the first example of a chatbot. Developed at the MIT between 1964 and 1966, it used to mimic a human conversation, and it may have tricked the users (at least for the first few interactions) that there was a human on the other side. In reality, the algorithm behind the early versions was relatively simple, as it simply repeated or reformulated some of the sentence of the user posing them as questions (to many it gave the impression of talking to a shrink), but keep in mind that we're still talking of a few years before the first video game was even created. Such achievements led to a lot of hyper-inflated optimism into AI for the time. A few examples of this early optimism:

- 1958: "Within ten years a digital computer will be the world's chess champion, and a digital computer will discover and prove an important new mathematical theorem" [6].

- 1965: "Machines will be capable, within twenty years, of doing any work a man can do" [7].

- 1967: "Within a generation the problem of creating 'artificial intelligence' will substantially be solved" [8].

- 1970: "In from three to eight years we will have a machine with the general intelligence of an average human being" [9].

Of course, things didn't go exactly that way. Around the half of the 1970s, most of the researchers realized that they had definitely underestimated the problem. The main issue was, of course, with the computing power of the time. By the end of the 1960s, researchers realized that training a network of perceptrons with multiple layers led to better results than training a single perceptron, and by the half of the 1970s, *back-propagation* (the building block of how networks "learn") was theorized. In other words, the basic shape of a modern neural network was already theorized in the mid-1970s. However, training a neural-like model required a lot of CPU power to perform the calculations required to converge toward an optimal solution, and such hardware power wouldn't have been available for the next 25–30 years.

The *reasoning as search* approach in the meantime faced the combinational explosion problem. Transforming a decision process into a graph search problem was OK for playing chess, proving a geometric theorem, or finding synonyms of words, but more complex real-world problems would have easily resulted in humongous graphs, as their complexity would grow exponentially with the number of inputs—that relegated AI mostly to toy projects within research labs rather than real-world applications.

Finally, researchers learned what became known as *Moravec's paradox*: it's really easy for a deterministic machine to prove a theorem or solve a geometry problem, but much harder to perform more "fuzzy" tasks such as recognizing a face or walking around without bumping into objects. Research funding drained when results failed to materialize.

AI experienced a resurgence in the 1980s under the form of *expert systems*. An expert system is a software that answers questions or interprets the content of a text within a specific domain of knowledge, applying inference rules derived from the knowledge of human experts. The formal representation of knowledge through relational and graph-based databases introduced in the late 1970s led to this new revolution in AI that focused on how to best represent human knowledge and how to infer decisions from it.

Expert systems went through another huge wave of optimism followed by another crash. While they were relatively good in providing answers to simple domain-specific questions, they were just as good as the knowledge provided by the human experts. That made them very expensive to maintain and update and very prone to errors whenever an input looked slightly different from what was provided in the knowledge base. They were useful in specific contexts, but they couldn't be scaled up to solve more general-purpose problems. The whole framework of logic-based AI came under increasing criticism during the 1990s. Many researchers argued that a truly intelligent machine should have been designed bottom-up rather than top-down. A machine can't make logical inference about rain and umbrellas if it doesn't know what those things or concepts actually mean or look like—in other words, if it can't perform some form of human-like *classification* based both on intuition and acquired experience.

Such reflections gradually led to a new interest in the machine learning side of AI, rather than the knowledge-based or symbolic approaches. Also, the hardware in the late 1990s was much better than what was available to the MIT researchers in the 1960s, and simple tasks of computer vision that proved incredibly challenging at the time, like recognizing handwritten letters or detecting simple objects, could be solved thanks to Moore's law, which states that the number of transistors in a chip doubles approximately each 18 months. And thanks to the Web and the huge amount of data it made available over the years and the increased ease at sharing this data.

Today the neural network is a ubiquitous component in machine learning and AI in general. It's important to note, however, that other approaches may still be relevant in some scenarios. Finding the quickest path by bike between your home and your office is still largely a graph search problem. Intent detection in unstructured text still relies on language models. Other problems, like some games or real-world simulations, may employ genetic algorithms. And some specific domains may still leverage expert systems. However, even when other algorithms are employed, neural networks nowadays often represent the "glue" to connect all the components. Different algorithms or networks are nowadays often modular blocks connected together through *data pipelines*.

Deep learning has become increasingly popular over the past decade, as better hardware and more data made it possible to train more data to bigger networks with more layers. Deep learning, under the hood, is the process of solving some of the common problems with earlier networks (like overfitting) by adding more neurons and more layers. Usually the accuracy of a network increases when you increase its number of layers and nodes, as the network will be better at spotting patterns in non-linear problems. However, deep learning may be plagued by some issues as well. One of them is the *vanishing gradient problem*, where gradients slowly shrink as they pass through more and more layers. Another more concrete issue is related to its environmental impact: while throwing more data and more neurons at a network and running more training iterations seems to make the network more accurate, it also represents a very power-hungry solution that cannot be sustainable for long-term growth.

1.2 Supervised and unsupervised learning

Now that the difference between artificial intelligence and machine learning is clear and we have got some context of how we have got where we are now, let's shift our focus to machine learning and the two main "learning" categories: supervised and unsupervised learning:

- We define as **supervised learning** the set of algorithms where a model is trained on a *dataset* that includes both example input data and the associated expected output.

- In **unsupervised learning,** on the other hand, we train models on datasets that don't include the expected outputs. In these algorithms, we expect the model to "figure out" patterns by itself.

When it comes to supervised learning, training a model usually consists in calculating a function $\bar{y} = f(\bar{x})$ that maps a given a vector of inputs $\bar{x}$ to a vector of outputs $\bar{y}$ such that the mean error between the predicted and the expected values is minimized. Some applications of supervised learning algorithms include

- Given a training set containing one million pictures of cats and one million pictures that don't feature cats, build a model that recognizes cats in previously unseen pictures. In this case, the training set will usually include a True/False label to tell whether the picture includes a cat. This is usually considered a **classification** problem—that is, given some input values and their labels (together called *training set*), you want your model to predict the correct *class*, or label—for example, "does/does not contain a cat." Or, if you provide the model with many examples of emails labelled as spam/not spam, you may train your classifier to detect spam on previously unseen emails.

- Given a training set containing the features of a large list of apartments in a city (size, location, construction year, etc.) together with their price, build a model that can predict the value of a new apartment on the market. This is usually considered a **regression** problem—that is, given a training set you want to train a model that predicts the best numeric approximation for a newly provided input in, for example, dollars, meters, or kilograms.

Unsupervised learning, on the other hand, is often used to solve problems whose goal is to find the underlying structure, distribution, or patterns in the data. Being provided with no expected labels, these are types of problems that come with no exact/correct answers nor comparison with expected values. Some examples of unsupervised learning problems include

- Given a large list of customers on an ecommerce website with the relevant input features (age, gender, address, list of purchases in the past year, etc.), find the optimal way to segment your customer base in order to plan several advertisement campaigns. This is usually considered a **clustering** problem—that is, given a set of inputs, find the best way to group them together.

- Given a user on a music streaming platform with its relevant features (age, gender, list of tracks listened in the past month, etc.), build a model that can recommend user profiles with similar musical taste. This is usually considered as a **recommender system**, or **association** problem—that is, a model that finds the nearest neighbors to a particular node.

Finally, there can be problems that sit halfway between supervised and unsupervised learning. Think of a large production database where some images are labelled (e.g., "cat," "dog," etc.) but some aren't—for example, because it's expensive to hire enough humans to manually label all the records or because the problem is very large and providing a full picture of all the possible labels is hard. In such cases, you may want to rely on hybrid implementations that use supervised learning to learn from the available labelled data and leverage unsupervised learning to find patterns in the unlabelled data.

In the rest of the book, we will mainly focus on *supervised learning*, since this category includes most of the neural architectures in use today, as well as all the regression problems. Some popular unsupervised learning algorithms will, however, be worth a mention, as they may be often used in symbiosis with supervised algorithms.

1.3 Preparing your tools

After so much talk about machine learning, let's introduce the tools that we'll be using through our journey. You won't need a Raspberry Pi (yet) during this chapter: as we cover the algorithms and the software tools used for machine learning, your own laptop will do the job.

Through the next sections, I'll assume that you have some knowledge/ experience with

- Any programming language (if you have experience with Python, even better). Python has become the most popular choice for machine learning over the past couple of years, but even if you don't have much experience with it, don't worry—it's relatively simple, and I'll try to comment the code as much as possible.

- High school (or higher) level of math. If you are familiar with calculus, statistics, and linear algebra, that's even better. If not, don't worry. Although some calculus and linear algebra concepts are required to grasp how machine learning works under the hood, I'll try not to dig too much into the theory, and whenever I mention gradients, tensors, or recall, I'll make sure to focus more on what they intuitively mean rather than their formal definition alone.

1.3.1 Software tools

We'll be using the following software tools through our journey:

- **The Python programming language** (version 3.6 or higher).

- **TensorFlow**, probably the most popular framework nowadays for building, training, and querying machine learning models.

- **Keras**, a very popular library for neural networks and regression models that easily integrates on top of TensorFlow.

- **numpy** and **pandas**, the most commonly used Python libraries, respectively, for numeric manipulations and data analysis.

- **matplotlib**, a Python library for plotting data and images.

- **seaborn**, a Python library often used for statistical data visualization.

- **jupyter**, a very popular solution for Python for prototyping through notebooks (and basically a standard de facto when it comes to data science in Python).

- **git**, we'll use it to download the sample datasets and notebooks from GitHub.

1.3.2 Setting up your environment

- Download and install git on your system, if it's not available already.

- Download and install a recent version of Python from `https://python.org/downloads`, if it's not already available on your system. Make sure that you use a version of Python greater than 3 (Python 2 is deprecated). Open a terminal and check that both the `python` and `pip` commands are present.

- (Optional) Create a new Python virtual environment. A virtual environment allows you to keep your machine learning setup separate from the main Python installation, without messing with any system-wide dependencies, and it also allows you to install Python packages in a non-privileged user space. You can skip this step if you prefer to install the dependencies system-wide (although you may need root/administrator privileges).

```
# Create a virtual environment under your home folder
python -m venv $HOME/venv
# Activate the environment
cd $HOME/venv
source bin/activate
# Whenever you are done, run 'deactivate'
# to go back to your standard environment
deactivate
```

- Install the dependencies (it may take a while depending on your connectivity and CPU power):

```
pip install tensorflow
pip install keras
pip install numpy
pip install pandas
pip install matplotlib
pip install jupyter
pip install seaborn
```

- Download the "mlbook-code" repository containing some of the datasets and code snippets that we'll be using through this book. We'll call <REPO_DIR> the directory where you have cloned the repository.

- Start the Jupyter server:

```
jupyter notebook
```

- Open http://localhost:8888 in your browser. You should see a login screen like the one shown in Figure 1-1. You can decide whether to authenticate using the token or set a password.

- Select a folder where you'd like to store your notebooks (we'll identify it as <NOTEBOOK_DIR> from now on), and create your first notebook. Jupyter notebooks are lists of cells; each of these cells can contain Python code, markdown elements, images, and so on. Start to get familiar with the environment, try to run some Python commands, and make sure that things work.

```
git clone https://github.com/BlackLight/mlbook-code
```

Now that all the tools are ready, let's get our hands dirty with some algorithms.

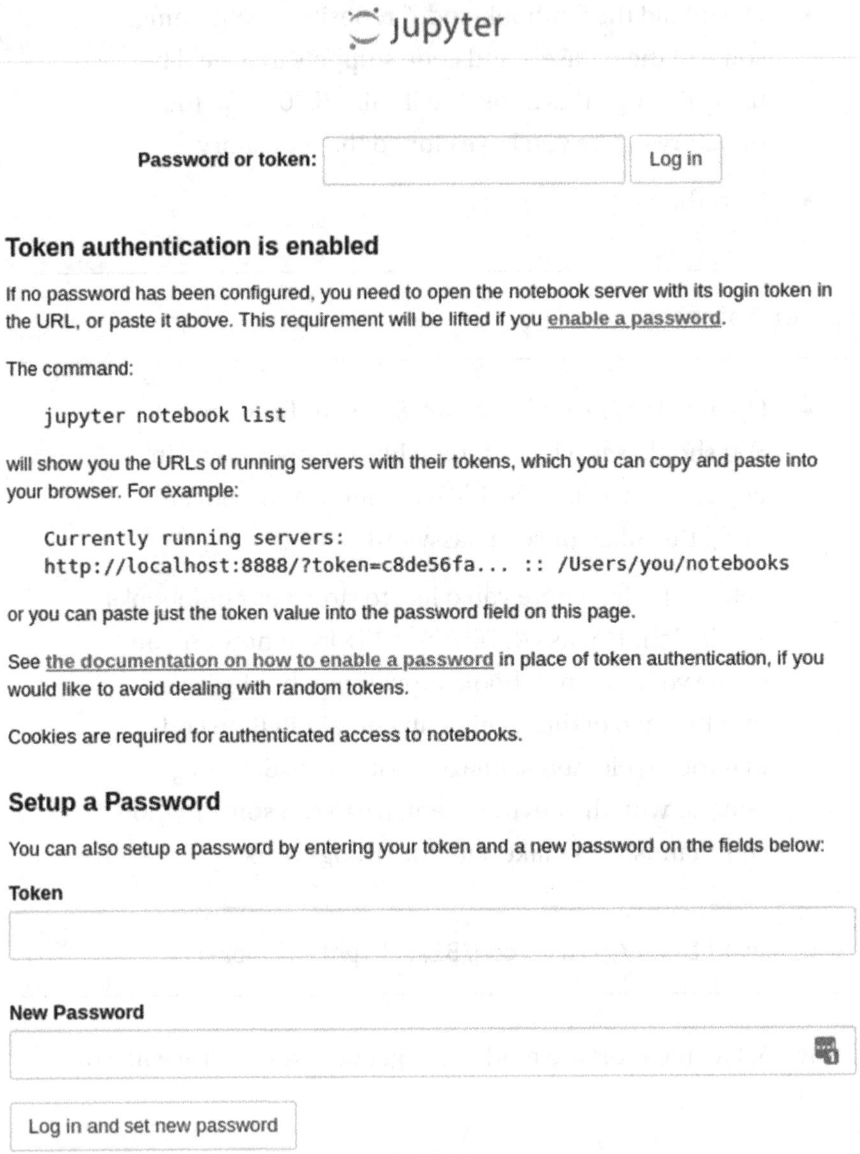

$\bigcirc$ jupyter

Password or token: [   ]   Log in

Token authentication is enabled

If no password has been configured, you need to open the notebook server with its login token in the URL, or paste it above. This requirement will be lifted if you enable a password.

The command:

```
jupyter notebook list
```

will show you the URLs of running servers with their tokens, which you can copy and paste into your browser. For example:

```
Currently running servers:
http://localhost:8888/?token=c8de56fa... :: /Users/you/notebooks
```

or you can paste just the token value into the password field on this page.

See the documentation on how to enable a password in place of token authentication, if you would like to avoid dealing with random tokens.

Cookies are required for authenticated access to notebooks.

Setup a Password

You can also setup a password by entering your token and a new password on the fields below:

Token

[   ]

New Password

[   ]

[Log in and set new password]

Figure 1-1. *Jupyter login screen at* $http://localhost:8888$

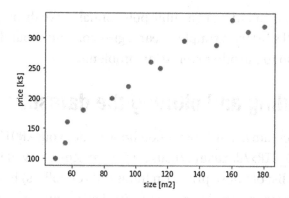

Figure 1-2. *Distribution of the house prices as a function of their size*

1.4 Linear regression

Linear regression is the first machine learning algorithm we'll encounter on our journey, as well as the most important. As we'll see, most of the supervised machine learning algorithms are variations of linear regression or applications of linear regression on scale. Linear regression is good for solving problems where you have some input data represented by n dimensions and you want to learn from their distribution in order to make predictions on future data points—for example, to predict the price of a house in a neighborhood or of a stock given a list of historical data. Linear regression is extensively used as a statistical tool also in finance, logistics, and economics to predict the price of a commodity, the demand in a certain period, or other macroeconomic variables. It's the building block of other types of regression—like logistic regression, which in turn is the building block of neural networks.

A regression model is called a *simple regression* model if the input data is represented by a single variable ($n = 1$) or *multivariate regression* if it operates on input data defined by multiple dimensions. It's called *linear regression* if its output is a line that best approximates the input data. Other types of regression exist as well—for instance, you'll have a *quadratic regression* if you try to fit a parabola instead of a line through your data, a *cubic regression* if you try to fit a cubic polynomial curve through your data, and so on. We'll start with simple linear regression and expand its basic mechanism also to the other regression problems.

1.4.1 Loading and plotting the dataset

To get started, create a new Jupyter notebook under your <NOTEBOOK_DIR> and load <REPO_DIR>/datasets/house-size-price-1.csv. It is a CSV file that contains a list of house prices (in thousands of dollars) in function of their size (in square meters) in a certain city. Let's suppose for now that the size is the only parameter that we've got, and we want to create a model trained on this data that predicts the price of a new house given its size.

The first thing you should do before jumping into defining any machine learning model is to visualize your data and try to understand what's the best model to use. This is how we load the CSV using pandas and visualize it using matplotlib:

```python
import pandas as pd

import matplotlib.pyplot as plt

# Download the CSV file from GitHub

csv_url = 'https://raw.githubusercontent.com/' +

          'BlackLight/mlbook-code/master/' +

          'datasets/house-size-price-1.csv'

data = pd.read_csv(csv_url)

# The first column contains the size in m2

size = data[columns[0]]

# The second column contains the price in thousands of dollars
```

```
price = data[columns[1]]
# Create a new figure and plot the data
fig = plt.figure()
plot = fig.add_subplot()
plot.set_xlabel(columns[0])
plot.set_ylabel(columns[1])
points = plot.scatter(size, price)
```

After running the content of your cell, you should see a graph like the one picture in Figure 1-2. You'll notice that the data is a bit scattered, but still it can be approximated well enough if we could fit a straight line through it. Our goal is now to find the line that best approximates our data.

1.4.2 The idea behind regression

Let's put our notebook aside for a moment and try to think which characteristic such a function should have. First, it must be a line; therefore, it must have a form like this:

$$h_\theta(x) = \theta_0 + \theta_1 x \qquad (1.1)$$

In Equation 1.1, x denotes the input data, excluding the output labels. In the case of the house size-price model, we have one input variable (the size) and one output variable (the price); therefore, both the input and output vectors have unitary size, but other models may have multiple input variables and/or multiple output variables. θ_0 and θ_1 are instead the numeric coefficients of the line. In particular, θ_0 tells where the line crosses the y axis and θ_1 tells us the direction of the line and how "steep" it is—it's often called the *slope* of the line. $h_\theta(x)$ is instead the function that our model will use for predictions based on the values of the vector $\bar{\theta}$ —also called *weights* of the model. In our problem, the inputs $\bar{x}$ and the expected outputs $\bar{y}$ are provided through the training set; therefore, the linear regression problem is a problem of finding the $\bar{\theta}$ parameters in the preceding equation such that $h_\theta(x)$ is a good approximation of the linear dependency between x and y. $h_\theta(x)$ is often denoted as *hypothesis function*, or simply *model*. The generic formula for a single-variable model of order n (linear for $n = 1$, quadratic for $n = 2$, etc.) will be

$$h_\theta\left(x\right)=\theta_0 +\theta_1 x+\theta_2 x^2 +...+\theta_n x^n = \sum_{i=0}^{n}\theta_i x^i \qquad (1.2)$$

Also, note that the "bar" or "superscript" on top of a symbol in this book will denote a *vector*. A vector is a fixed-size list of numeric elements, so $\bar{\theta}$ is actually a more compact way to write $[\theta_0, \theta_1]$ or $[\theta_0...\theta_n]$.

So how can we formalize the intuitive concept of "good enough linear approximation" into an algorithm? The intuition is to choose the $\bar{\theta}$ parameters such that their associated $h_\theta(x)$ function is "close enough" to the provided samples y for the given values of x. More formally, we want to minimize the *squared mean error* between the sampled values y and the predicted values $h_\theta(x)$ for all the m data points provided in the training set—if the error between the predicted and the actual values is low, then the model is performing well:

$$\min_{\theta_0 ,\theta_1}\frac{1}{2m}\sum_{i=1}^{m}\left(h_\theta\left(x_i\right)-y_i\right)^2 \qquad (1.3)$$

Let's rephrase the argument of the preceding formula as a function of the parameters $\bar{\theta}$:

$$J\left(\bar{\theta}\right)=\frac{1}{2m}\sum_{i=1}^{m}\left(h_\theta\left(x_i\right)-y_i\right)^2 \qquad (1.4)$$

The function J is also called **cost function** (or **loss function**), since it expresses the cost (or, in this case, the approximation error) of a line associated to a particular selection of the $\bar{\theta}$ parameters. Finding the best linear approximation for your data is therefore a problem of finding the values of $\bar{\theta}$ that minimize the preceding cost function (i.e., the sum of the mean squared errors between samples and predictions). Note the difference between $h_\theta(x)$ and $J(\bar{\theta})$: the former is our *model hypothesis*, that is, the prediction function of the model expressed by its vector of parameters $\bar{\theta}$ and with x as a variable. $J(\bar{\theta})$ is instead the cost function and the parameters $\bar{\theta}$ are the variables, and our goal is to find the values of $\bar{\theta}$ that minimize this function in order to calculate the best $h_\theta(x)$. If we want to start formalizing the procedure, we can say that the problem of finding the optimal regression model can be expressed as follows:

- Start with a set of initial parameters $\bar{\theta} = [\theta_0, \theta_1, ..., \theta_n]$, with n being the order of your regression ($n = 1$ for linear, $n = 2$ for quadratic, etc.).

- Use those values to formulate a hypothesis $h_\theta(x)$ as shown in Equation 1.2.

- Calculate the cost function $J(\bar{\theta})$ associated to that hypothesis as shown in Equation 1.4.

- Keep changing the values of $\bar{\theta}$ until we converge on a point that minimizes the cost function.

Now that it's clear how a regression algorithm is modelled and how to measure how good it approximates the data, let's cover how to implement the last point in the preceding list—that is, the actual "learning" phase.

1.4.3 Gradient descent

Hopefully so many mentions of "error minimization" have rung a bell if you have some memory of calculus! The *differential* (or *derivative*) is the mathematical instrument leveraged in most of the minimization/ maximization problems. In particular:

- The *first derivative* of a function tells us whether that function is increasing or decreasing around a certain point or it is "still" (i.e., the point is a local minimum/maximum or an inflection point). It can be geometrically visualized as the slope of the *tangent* line to the function in a certain point. If we name $f'(x)$ the first derivative of a function $f(x)$ (with $x \in \Re$ for now), then its value in a point x_0 will be (assuming that the function is *differentiable* in x_0)

$$f'(x_0) \begin{cases} > 0 \text{ if the curve is increasing} \\ < 0 \text{ if the curve is decreasing} \\ = 0 \text{ if } x_0 \text{ is a min/ max/ flex} \end{cases} \quad (1.5)$$

- The *second derivative* of a function tells us the "concavity" of that function around a certain point, that is, whether the curve is facing "up" or "down" around that point. The second derivative $f''(x)$ around a given point x_0 will be

$$f''(x_0) \begin{cases} > 0 \text{ if the curve faces up} \\ < 0 \text{ if the curve faces down} \\ = 0 \text{ if } x_0 \text{ is an inflection point} \end{cases} \quad (1.6)$$

By combining these two instruments, we can find out, given a certain point on a surface, in which direction the minimum of that function is. In other words, minimizing the cost function $J(\bar{\theta})$ is a problem of finding a vector of values $\bar{\theta}^* = [\theta_0, \theta_1, \ldots, \theta_n]$ such that the first derivative of J for $\bar{\theta}^*$ is zero (or close enough to zero) and its second derivative is positive (i.e., the point is a local minimum). In most of the algorithms in this book, we won't actually need the second derivative (many of today's popular machine learning models are built around *convex* cost functions, i.e., cost functions with one single point of minimum), but applications with higher polynomial models may leverage the idea of concavity behind the second derivative to tell whether a point is a minimum, a maximum, or an inflection.

This intuition works for the case with a single variable. However, J is a function of a vector of parameters $\bar{\theta}$, whose length is 2 for linear regression, 3 for quadratic, and so on. For multivariate functions, the concept of *gradient* is used instead of the derivative used for univariate functions. The gradient of a multivariate function (usually denoted by the symbol ∇) is the vector of the *partial derivatives* (conventionally denoted by the ∂ symbol) of that function calculated against each of the variables. In the case of our cost function, its gradient will be

$$\nabla J(\bar{\theta}) = \begin{bmatrix} \dfrac{\partial}{\partial \theta_0} J(\bar{\theta}) \\ \vdots \\ \dfrac{\partial}{\partial \theta_n} J(\bar{\theta}) \end{bmatrix} \tag{1.7}$$

In practice, a partial derivative is the process of calculating the derivative of a multivariate function assuming that only one of its variables is the actual variable and the others are constants.

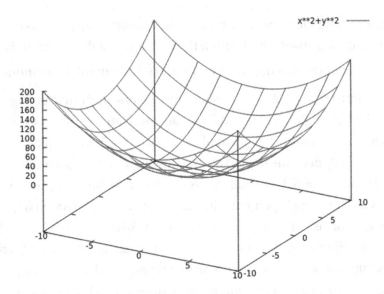

Figure 1-3. *Typical shape of the cost function for a linear regression model: a paraboloid in a 3D space*

The gradient vector indicates the direction in which an *n*-dimensional curve is increasing around a certain point and "how fast" it is increasing. In the case of linear regression with one input variable, we have seen in Equation 1.4 that the cost function is a function of two variables (θ_0 and θ_1) and that it is a quadratic function. In fact, by combining Equations 1.1 and 1.4, we can derive the cost function for linear regression with univariate input:

$$J\left(\theta_0,\theta_1\right)=\frac{1}{2m}\sum_{i=1}^{m}\left(\theta_0+\theta_1 x_i - y_i\right)^2 \qquad (1.8)$$

This surface can be represented in a 3D space like a paraboloid (a bowl shape that you get if you rotate 360 degrees a parabola around its axis, as shown in Figure 1-3). That puts us in a relatively lucky spot. Just like a parabola, a paraboloid has only one minimum—that is, only one point where its vector gradient is zero, and that point also happens to be the global minimum. It means that if we start with some random values for $\bar{\theta}$ and then start "walking" in the opposite direction of the gradient in that point, we should eventually end up in the optimal point—that is, the vector of parameters $\bar{\theta}^*$ that we can plug in our hypothesis function $h_\theta(x)$ to get good predictions. Remember that, given a point on a surface, the gradient vector tells you in which direction the function goes "up." If you go in its opposite direction, you will be going down. And if your surface has the shape of a bowl, if you keep going down, from wherever you are on the surface, you will eventually get to the bottom. If you instead use more complex types of regression (quadratic, cubic, etc.), you may not always be so lucky—you could get stuck in a local minimum, which does not represent the overall minimum of the function. So, assuming that we are happy as soon as we start converging toward a minimum, the *gradient descent* algorithm can be expressed as a procedure where we start by initially picking up random values for $\bar{\theta}$, and then at each step k, we update these values through the following formula:

$$\theta_i^{(k+1)} = \theta_i^{(k)} - \alpha \frac{\partial}{\partial \theta_i} J\left(\theta_0^{(k)}, \theta_1^{(k)}\right) \text{ for } i = 0,1 \tag{1.9}$$

Or, in vectorial form:

$$\bar{\theta}^{(k+1)} = \bar{\theta}^{(k)} - \alpha \nabla J\left(\bar{\theta}^{(k)}\right) \tag{1.10}$$

α is a parameter between zero and one known as the **learning rate** of the machine learning model, and it expresses *how fast* the model should learn from new data—in other words, how big the "leaps" down the direction of the gradient vector should be. A large value of α would result in a model that could learn fast at the beginning, but that could overshoot the minimum or "miss the stop"—at some point, it could land near the minimum of the cost function and could miss it by taking a longer step, resulting in some "bounces" back and forth before converging. A small value of α, on the other hand, may be slow at learning at the beginning and could take more iterations, but it's basically guaranteed to converge without too many bounces around the minimum.

To use a metaphor, performing learning through gradient descent is like pushing a ball blindfolded down a valley. First, you have to figure out in which direction the bottom of the valley is, using the direction of the gradient vector as a compass. Then, you have to find out how much force you want to apply to the ball to get it to the bottom. If you push it with a lot of force, it may reach the bottom faster, but it may go back and forth a few times before settling. Instead, if you only let gravity do its work, the ball may take longer to get to the bottom, but once it's there, it's unlikely to swing too much. In most of today's applications, the learning rate is dynamic: you may usually want a higher value of α in the first phase (when your model doesn't know much yet about the data) and lower it toward the end (when your model has already seen a significant number of data points and/or the cost function is converging). Some popular algorithms nowadays also perform some kind of learning rate *shuffling* in case they get stuck.

We may want to also set an *exit condition* for the algorithm: in case it doesn't converge on a vector of parameters that nullifies the cost function, for example, we may want to still exit if the gradient of the cost function is close enough to zero, or there hasn't been a significant improvement from the previous step, or the corresponding model is already good enough at approximating our problem.

By combining Equations 1.8 and 1.9 and applying the differentiation rules, we can derive the exact update steps for θ_0 and θ_1 in the case of linear regression:

$$\theta_0^{(k+1)} = \theta_0^{(k)} - \frac{\alpha}{m}\sum_{i=1}^{m}\left(\theta_0^{(k)} + \theta_1^{(k)}x_i - y_i\right) \tag{1.11}$$

$$\theta_1^{(k+1)} = \theta_1^{(k)} - \frac{\alpha}{m} \sum_{i=1}^{m} \left(\theta_0^{(k)} + \theta_1^{(k)} x_i - y_i \right) x_i \qquad (1.12)$$

So the full algorithm for linear regression can be summarized as follows:

1. Pick random values for θ_0 and θ_1.

2. Keep updating θ_0 and θ_1 through, respectively, Equations 1.11 and 1.12.

3. Terminate either after performing a preset number of training iterations (often called *epochs*) or when convergence is achieved (i.e., no significant improvement has been measured on a certain step compared to the step before).

There are many tools and library that can perform efficient regression, so it's uncommon that you will have to implement the algorithm from scratch. However, since the preceding steps are known, it's relatively simple to write a univariate linear regression algorithm in Python with numpy alone:

```python
import numpy as np
def gradient_descent(x, y, theta, alpha):
    m = len(x)
    new_theta = np.zeros(2)
    # Perform the gradient descent on theta
    for i in range(m):
        new_theta[0] += theta[0] + theta[1]*x[i] - y[i]
```

```
        new_theta[1] += (theta[0] + theta[1]*x[i] - y[i]) *
        x[i]
    return theta - (alpha/m) * new_theta
def train(x, y, steps, alpha=0.001):
    # Initialize theta randomly
    theta = np.random.randint(low=0, high=10, size=2)
    # Perform the gradient descent <steps> times
    for i in range(steps):
        theta = gradient_descent(x, y, theta, alpha)
    # Return the linear function associated to theta
    return lambda x: theta[0] + theta[1] * x
```

1.4.4 Input normalization

Let's pick up our notebook where we left it. We should now have a clear idea of how to train a regression model to predict the price of a house given its size. We will use TensorFlow+Keras for defining and training the model.

Before proceeding, however, it's important to spend a word about input normalization (or **feature scaling**). It's very important that your model is robust enough even if some data is provided in different units than those used in the training set or some arbitrary constant is added or multiplied to your inputs. That's why it's important to normalize your inputs before feeding it to any machine learning model. Not only that, but if the inputs are well distributed within a specific range centered around the origin, the model will be much faster at converging than if you provide raw inputs with no specific range. Worse, a non-normalized training set could often result in a cost function that doesn't converge at all.

Input normalization is usually done by applying the following transformation:

$$\hat{x}_i = \frac{x_i - \mu}{\sigma} \text{ for } i = 1, \ldots, m \tag{1.13}$$

where x_i is the i-th element of your m-long input vector, μ is the arithmetic mean of the vector $\bar{x}$ of the inputs, and σ is its standard deviation:

$$\mu = \frac{1}{m} \sum_{i=1}^{m} x_i \tag{1.14}$$

$$\sigma = \sqrt{\frac{1}{m} \sum_{i=1}^{m} (x_i - \mu)^2} \tag{1.15}$$

By applying Equation 1.13 to our inputs, we basically transpose the input values around the zero and group most of them around the $[-\sigma, \sigma]$ range. When predicting values, we instead want to denormalize the provided output, which can easily be done by deriving x_i from Equation 1.13:

$$x_i = \sigma \hat{x}_i + \mu \tag{1.16}$$

It's quite easy to write these functions in Python and insert them in our notebook. First, get the dataset stats using the pandas describe method:

```
dataset_stats = data.describe()
```

Then define the functions to normalize and denormalize your data:

```
def normalize(x, stats):
    return (x - stats['mean']) / stats['std']
def denormalize(x, stats):
    return stats['std'] * x + stats['mean']
norm_size = normalize(size, dataset_stats['size'])
norm_price = normalize(price, dataset_stats['price'])
```

1.4.5 Defining and training the model

Defining and training a linear regression model with TensorFlow+Keras is quite easy:

```
from tensorflow.keras.experimental import LinearModel
model = LinearModel(units=1, activation='linear',
dtype='float32')
model.compile(optimizer='rmsprop', loss='mse',
metrics=['mse'])
history = model.fit(norm_size, norm_price, epochs=1000,
verbose=0)
```

There are quite a few things happening here:

- First, we define a `LinearModel` with one input variable (`units=1`), `linear` activation function (i.e., the output value of the model is returned directly without being transformed by a non-linear output function), and with `float32` numeric type.

- Then, we `compile` the model, making it ready to be trained. The `optimizer` in Keras does many things. A deep understanding of the optimizers would require a dedicated chapter, but for sake of keeping it brief, we will quickly cover what they do as we use them. `rmsprop` initializes the learning rate and gradually adjusts it over the training iterations as a function of the recent gradients [10]. By default, `rmsprop` is initialized with `learning_rate=0.001`. You can, however, try and tweak it and see how/if it affects your model:

```
from tensorflow.keras.optimizers import RMSprop
rmsprop = RMSprop(learning_rate=0.005)
model.compile(optimizer=rmsprop, loss='mse', metrics=['mse'])
```

- Other common optimizers include
  - SGD, or *stochastic gradient descent*, which implements the gradient descent algorithm described in Equation 1.9 with few optimizations and tweaks, such as learning rate decay and Nesterov momentum [11]

- – adam, an algorithm for first-order gradient-based optimization
    that has recently gain quite some momentum, especially in
    deep learning [12]

  – nadam, which implements support for Nesterov momentum
    on top of the adam algorithm [13]

- Feel free to experiment with different optimizers
  and different learning rates to see how it affects the
  performance of your model.

- The loss parameter defines the *loss/cost function* to
  be optimized. mse means *mean squared error*, as we
  have defined it in Equation 1.4. Other common loss
  functions include

  – mae, or *mean absolute error*—similar to mse, but it uses the
    absolute value of $h(x_i) - y_i$ in Equation 1.4 instead of the
    squared value.

  – mape, or *mean absolute percentage error*—similar to mae, but it
    uses the percentage of the absolute error compared to the
    previous iteration as a target metric.

  – mean_squared_logarithmic_error—similar to mse, but it uses
    the logarithm of the mean squared error (useful if your curve
    has exponential features).

  – Several *cross-entropy* loss functions (e.g., categorical_cros-
    sentropy, sparse_categorical_crossentropy, and binary_
    crossentropy), often used for classification problems.

- The metrics attribute is a list that identifies the metrics
  to be used to evaluate the performance of your model.
  In this example, we use the same metric used as the
  loss/cost function (the mean squared error), but other
  metrics can be used as well. A metric is conceptually

similar to the loss/cost function, except that the result
of the metric function is only used to evaluate the
model, not to train it. You can also use multiple metrics
if you want your model to be evaluated according to
multiple features. Other common metrics include

- mae, or *mean absolute error.*

- accuracy and its derived metrics (`binary_accuracy`, `categor-
  ical_accuracy`, `sparse_categorical_accuracy`, `top_k_cat-
  egorical_accuracy`, etc.). Accuracy is often used in
  classification problems, and it expresses the fraction of correctly labelled items in the training set over the total amount
  of items in the training set.

- Custom metrics can also be defined. As we'll see later when
  we tackle classification problems, precision, recall, and F1
  score are quite popular evaluation metrics. These aren't part
  of the core framework (yet?), but they can easily be defined.

- Finally, we *train* our model on the normalized data
  from the previous step using the `fit` function. The
  first argument of the function will be the vector of
  input values, the second argument will be the vector
  of expected output values, and then we specify the
  number of **epochs**, that is, training iterations that we
  want to perform on this data.

The **epochs** value depends a lot on your dataset. The cumulative
number of input samples you will present to your model is given by $\times$
epochs, where m is the size of your dataset. In our case, we've got a relatively
small dataset, which means that you want to run more training epochs to
make sure that your model has seen enough data. If you have larger training
sets, however, you may want to run less training iterations. The risk of
running too many training iterations on the same batch of data, as we will

see later, is to *overfit* your data, that is, to create a model that closely mimics the expected outputs if presented with values close enough to those it's been trained on, but inaccurate over data points it hasn't been trained on.

1.4.6 Evaluating your model

Now that we have defined and trained our model and we have a clear idea of how to measure its performance, let's take a look at how its primary metric (mean squared error) has improved during the training phase:

```
epochs = history.epoch

loss = history.history['loss']

fig = plt.figure()

plot = fig.add_subplot()

plot.set_xlabel('epoch')

plot.set_ylabel('loss')

plot.plot(epochs, loss)
```

You should see a plot like the one shown in Figure 1-4. You'll notice that the loss curve goes drastically down—which is good; it means that our model is actually learning when we input it with data points, without getting stuck in gradient "valleys." It also means that the learning rate was well calibrated—if your learning rate is too high, the model may not necessarily converge, and if it's too low, then it may still be on its way toward convergence after many training epochs. Also, there is a short tail around 0.07. This is also good: it means that our model has converged over the last iterations.

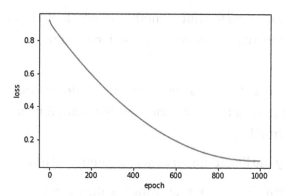

Figure 1-4. *Linear regression model loss evolution over training*

If the tail is too long, it means that you have trained your model for too many epochs, and you may want to reduce either the number of epochs or the size of your training set to prevent overfit. If the tail is too short or there's no tail at all, your model hasn't been trained on enough data points, and probably you will have to either increase the size of your training set or the number of epochs to gain accuracy.

You can (read: should) also evaluate your model on some data that isn't necessarily part of your training set to check how well the model performs on new data points. We will dig deeper on how to split your *training set* and *test set* later. For now, given the relatively small dataset, we can evaluate the model on the dataset itself through the evaluate function:

```
model.evaluate(norm_size, norm_price)
```

You should see some output like this:

```
0s 2ms/step - loss: 0.0733 - mse: 0.0733
[0.0733143612742424, 0.0733143612742424]
```

The returned vector contains the values of the loss function and metric functions, respectively—in our case, since we used mse for both, they are the same.

Finally, let's see how the linear model actually looks against our dataset and let's start to use it to make predictions. First, define a `predict` function that will

1. Take a list of house `sizes` as input and normalize them against the mean and standard deviation of your training set

2. Query the linear model to get the predicted prices

3. Denormalize the output using the mean and standard deviation of the training set to convert the prices in thousands of dollars

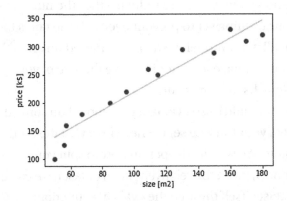

Figure 1-5. *Plotting your linear model against the dataset*

```
def predict_prices(*x):

    x = normalize(x, dataset_stats['size'])

    return denormalize(model.predict(x), dataset_
    stats['price'])
```

And let's use this function to get some predictions of house prices:

```
predict_prices(90)
array([[202.53752]], dtype=float32)
```

The "predict" function will return a list of output associated to your inputs, where each item is a vector containing the predicted values (in this case, vectors of unitary size, because our model has a single output unit). If you look back at Figure 1-2, you'll see that a predicted price of 202.53752 for *size* = 90 doesn't actually look that far from the distribution of the data—and that's good. To visualize how our linear model looks against our dataset, let's plot the dataset again and let's calculate two points on the model in order to draw the line:

```
# Draw the linear regression model as a line between the first and
# the last element of the numeric series. x will contain the lowest
# and highest size (assumption: the series is ordered) and y will
# contain the price predictions for those inputs.
x = [size[0], size.iat[-1]]
y = [p[0] for p in predict_prices(*x)]
# Create a new figure and plot both the input data points and the
# linear model approximation.
fig = plt.figure()
```

```
data_points = fig.add_subplot()

data_points.scatter(size, price)

data_points.set_xlabel(columns[0])

data_points.set_ylabel(columns[1])

model_line = fig.add_subplot()

model_line.plot(x, y, 'r')
```

The output of the preceding code will hopefully look like Figure 1-5. That tells us that the line calculated by the model isn't actually that far from our data. If you happen to see that your line is far from the model, it probably means that you haven't trained your model on enough data, or the learning rate is too high/too low, or that there's no strong linear correlation between the metrics in your dataset and maybe you need a higher polynomial model, or maybe that there are many "outliers" in your model—that is, many data points outside of the main distribution that "drag" the line out.

1.4.7 Saving and loading your model

Your model is now loaded in memory in your notebook, but you will lose it once the Jupyter notebook stops. You may want to save it to the filesystem, so you can recover it later without going through the training phase again. Or you can include it in another script to make predictions. Luckily, it's quite easy to save and load Keras models on the filesystem—the following examples, however, will assume that you are using a version of TensorFlow \geq 2.0:

```python
def model_save(model_dir, overwrite=True):
    import json
    import os
    os.makedirs(model_dir, exist_ok=True)
    # The TensorFlow model save won't keep track of the labels of
    # your model. It's usually a good practice to store them in a
    # separate JSON file.
    labels_file = os.path.join(model_dir, 'labels.json')
    with open(labels_file, 'w') as f:
        f.write(json.dumps(list(columns)))
    # Also, you may want to keep track of the x and y mean and
    # standard deviation to correctly normalize/denormalize your
    # data before/after feeding it to the model.
    stats = [
        dict(dataset_stats['size']),
        dict(dataset_stats['price']),
    ]
    stats_file = os.path.join(model_dir, 'stats.json')
    with open(stats_file, 'w') as f:
        f.write(json.dumps(stats))
        # Then, save the TensorFlow model using the save primitive
        model.save(model_dir, overwrite=overwrite)
```

You can then load the model in another notebook, script, application, and so on (bindings of TensorFlow are available for most of the programming languages in use nowadays) and use it for your predictions:

```python
def model_load(model_dir):
    import json
    import os
    from tensorflow.keras.models import load_model
    labels = []
    labels_file = os.path.join(model_dir, 'labels.json')
    if os.path.isfile(labels_file):
        with open(labels_file) as f:
            labels = json.load(f)
    stats = []
    stats_file = os.path.join(model_dir, 'stats.json')
    if os.path.isfile(stats_file):
        with open(stats_file) as f:
            stats = json.load(f)
    m = load_model(model_dir)
    return m, stats, labels
model, stats, labels = model_load(model_dir)
price = predict_prices(90)
```

1.5 Multivariate linear regression

So far we have explored linear regression models with one single input and output variable. Real-world regression problems are usually more complex, and the output features are usually expressed as a function of multiple variables. The price of a house, for instance, won't depend only on its size but also on its construction year, number of bedrooms, presence of extras such as garden or terrace, distance from the city center, and so on. In such a generic case, we express each input data point as a vector $\bar{x} = (x_1, x_2, \ldots, x_n) \in \mathfrak{R}^n$, and the regression expression seen in Equation 1.2 is reformulated as

$$h_\theta(\bar{x}) = \theta_0 + \theta_1 x_1 + \theta_2 x_2 + \ldots + \theta_n x_n = \theta_0 + \sum_{i=1}^{n} \theta_i x_i \qquad (1.17)$$

By convention, the input vector in case of multivariate regression is rewritten as $\bar{x} = (x_0, x_1, x_2, \ldots, x_n) \in \mathfrak{R}^{n+1}$, with $x_0 = 1$, so the preceding expression can be written more compactly as

$$h_\theta(\bar{x}) = \sum_{i=0}^{n} \theta_i x_i \qquad (1.18)$$

Or, by using the vectorial notation, the hypothesis function can be written as the *scalar product* between the vector of parameters $\bar{\theta}$ and the vector of features $\bar{x}$:

$$h_\theta(\bar{x}) = [\theta_0, \ldots, \theta_n] \begin{bmatrix} x_0 \\ \vdots \\ x_n \end{bmatrix} = \bar{\theta}^T \bar{x} \qquad (1.19)$$

Keep in mind that, by convention, vectors are represented as *columns* of values. The ^{T} notation denotes the *transposed* vector, so the vector represented as a row. By multiplying a row vector for a column vector, you get the *scalar product* of the two vectors, so $\bar{\theta}^T \bar{x}$ is a compact way to represent the scalar product of $\bar{\theta}$ into $\bar{x}$.

So the mean squared error cost function in Equation 1.8 can be rewritten in the multivariate case as

$$J(\bar{\theta}) = \frac{1}{2m} \sum_{i=1}^{m} \left(\sum_{j=0}^{n} \theta_j x_j^{(i)} - y^{(i)} \right)^2 \qquad (1.20)$$

Or, using the vectorial notation:

$$J(\bar{\theta}) = \frac{1}{2m} \sum_{i=1}^{m} \left(\bar{\theta}^T \bar{x}^{(i)} - y^{(i)} \right)^2 \qquad (1.21)$$

Since the inputs are no longer unitary, we are no longer talking of lines on a plane, but of *hyper-surfaces* in an n-dimensional space—they are a 1D line in a 2D space defined by one variable, a 2D plane in a 3D space defined by two variables, a 3D space in a 4D space defined by three variables, and so on. The cost function, on its side, will have $\bar{\theta} = (\theta_0, \theta_1, \ldots, \theta_n) \in \mathfrak{R}^{n+1}$ parameters—while it was a paraboloid surface in a 3D space in the univariate case, it will be an $n + 1$-dimensional surface in the case of n input features. This makes the multivariate case harder to visualize than the univariate, but we can still rely on our performance metrics to evaluate how well the model is doing or break down the linear n-dimensional surface by feature to analyze how each variable performs against the output feature.

By applying the generic vectorial equation for gradient descent shown in Equation 1.10, we can also rewrite the parameters' update formulas in Equations 1.11 and 1.12 in the following way (remember that $x_0 = 1$ by convention):

$$\theta_j^{(k+1)} = \theta_j^{(k)} - \frac{\alpha}{m} \sum_{i=1}^{m} \left(\bar{\theta}^T \bar{x}^{(i)} - y^{(i)} \right) x_j^{(i)} \tag{1.22}$$

We should now have all the tools also to write a multivariate regression algorithm with numpy alone:

```python
import numpy as np
def gradient_descent(x, y, theta, alpha):
    m = len(x)
    n = len(theta)
    new_theta = np.zeros(n)
    # Perform the gradient descent on theta
    for i in range(m):
        # s = theta[0] + (theta[1]*x[1] + .. + theta[n]*x[n]) -
        y[i]
        s = theta[0]
        for j in range(1, n):
            s += theta[j]*x[i][j-1]
        s -= y[i]
        new_theta[0] += s
        for j in range(1, n):
```

```
            new_theta[j] += s * x[i][j-1]
    return theta - (alpha/m) * new_theta
def train(x, y, steps, alpha=0.001):
    # Initialize theta randomly
    theta = np.random.randint(low=0, high=10,
    size=len(x[0])+1)
    # Perform the gradient descent <steps> times
    for i in range(steps):
        theta = gradient_descent(x, y, theta, alpha)
    # Return the linear function associated to theta
    def model(x):
        y = theta[0]
        for i in range(len(theta)-1):
            y += theta[i+1] * x[i]
        return y
    return model
```

These changes will make the linear regression algorithm analyzed for the univariate case work also in the generic multivariate case.

In the preceding code, I have expanded all the vectorial operations into for statements for sake of clarity, but keep in mind that most of the real regression algorithms out there perform vector sums and scalar products using native vectorial operations if available. You should have noticed by now that the gradient descent is a quite computationally expensive procedure. The algorithm goes over an *m*-sized dataset for *epochs* times and performs a few vector sums and scalar products each time, and each dataset item consists of n features. Things get even more computationally expensive once you perform gradient descent on multiple nodes, like in a neural network. Expressing the preceding steps in vectorial form allows to take advantage of some optimizations and parallelizations available either in the hardware or the software. I'll leave it as a take-home exercise to write the preceding n-dimensional gradient descent algorithm using vectorial primitives.

Before jumping into a practical example, let me spend a few words on two quite important topics in multi-feature problems: *feature selection* and *training/test set split*.

1.5.1 Redundant features

Adding more input features to your model will usually make your model more accurate in real-world examples. In the first regression problem we have solved, our model could predict the price of a house solely based on its size. We know by intuition that adding more features from real-world examples usually would make a price prediction more accurate. We know by intuition that if we also input features such as the year of construction of the house, the average price of the houses on that road, the presence of balconies or gardens, or the distance from the city center, we may get more accurate predictions. However, there is a limit to that. It is quite important that the features that you feed to your model are *linearly independent* from each other. Given a list of vectors $[\bar{x}_1, \bar{x}_2, ..., \bar{x}_m]$, a vector $\bar{x}_i$ in this list is defined as *linearly dependent* if it can be written as

$$\bar{x}_i = \sum_{j=1}^{m} k_j \bar{x}_j \qquad (1.23)$$

with $k = [k_1, k_2, \ldots, k_m] \in \mathfrak{R}^m$. In other words, if a feature can be expressed as a linear combination of any other number of features, then that feature is *redundant*. Example of redundant features include

- The same price expressed both in euros and in dollars

- The same distance expressed both in meters and in feet or in meters and kilometers

- A dataset that contains the net weight, the tare weight, and the gross weight of a product

- A dataset that contains the base price, the VAT rate, and the final price of a product

The preceding scenarios are all examples of features that are linear combinations of other features. You should remove all the redundant features from your dataset before feeding it to a model; otherwise, the predictions of your model will be skewed, or *biased*, toward the features that make up the derived feature(s). There are two ways of doing this:

1. *Manually*: Look at your data, and try to understand if there are any attributes that are redundant—that is, features that are linear combinations of other features.

2. *Analytically*: You will have m inputs in your dataset, each represented by n features. You can arrange them into an $m \times n$ matrix $X \in \mathfrak{R}^{m \times n}$. The **rank** of this matrix, $\rho(X)$, is defined as its number of linearly independent vectors (rows or columns). We can say that our dataset has no redundant features if its associated matrix X is such that

$$\rho(X) = \min(m, n) \tag{1.24}$$

If $\rho(X) = \min(m,n)-1$, then the dataset has one linearly dependent vector. If $\rho(X) = \min(m,n)-2$, then it has two linearly dependent vectors, and so on. Both numpy and scipy have built-in methods to calculate the rank of a matrix, so that may be a good way to go if you want to double-check that there are no redundant features in your dataset.

It's also equally important to try and remove duplicate rows in your dataset, as they could "pull" your model in some specific ranges. However, the impact of duplicate rows in a dataset won't be as bad as duplicate columns if $m \gg n$—that is, if the number of data samples is much greater than the number of features.

1.5.2 Principal component analysis

An analytical (and easy to automate) way to remove redundant features from your training set is to perform what's known as *principal component analysis,* or *PCA*. PCA is especially useful when you have a really high number of input features and performing a manual analysis of the functional dependencies could be cumbersome. PCA is an algorithm for *feature extraction*, that is, it reduces the number of dimensions in an n-dimensional input space A by mapping the points in A to a new k-dimensional space A', with $k \leq n$, such that the features in A' are *linearly independent* from each other—or, in other words, they are *orthogonal* to each other.

The math behind PCA may seem a bit hard at a first look, but it relies on a quite intuitive geometric idea, so bear with me the next couple of formulas.

The first step in PCA is *feature normalization,* as we have seen it in Equation 1.13:

$$\hat{x}_i = \frac{x_i - \mu_x}{\sigma_x} \text{ for } i = 1,\ldots,n \qquad (1.25)$$

with μ_x denoting the arithmetic mean of $\bar{x}$ and σ_x its standard deviation.

Then, given a normalized training set with input features $\bar{x} = [x_1, x_2, \ldots, x_n]$, we calculate the *covariance matrix* of $\bar{x}$ as

$$cov(\bar{x},\bar{x}) = (\bar{x} - \mu_x)(\bar{x} - \mu_x)^T$$

$$= \begin{bmatrix} (x_1 - \mu_x)(x_1 - \mu_x) & \cdots & (x_1 - \mu_x)(x_n - \mu_x) \\ (x_2 - \mu_x)(x_1 - \mu_x) & \cdots & (x_2 - \mu_x)(x_n - \mu_x) \\ \vdots & & \vdots \\ (x_n - \mu_x)(x_1 - \mu_x) & \cdots & (x_n - \mu_x)(x_n - \mu_x) \end{bmatrix} \quad (1.26)$$

You may recall from linear algebra that the product of two vectors in the form row into column, $\bar{x}^T\bar{y}$, is what's usually called *scalar product* or *dot product* and it returns a single real number, while the product of two vectors in the form column into row, $\bar{x}\bar{y}^T$, returns an $n \times n$ sized matrix, and that's what we get with the preceding covariance matrix. The intuition behind the covariance matrix of a vector with itself is to have a geometrical representation of the input distribution—it's like a multi-dimensional extension of the concept of variance in the case of one dimension.

We then proceed with calculating the *eigenvectors* of $cov(\bar{x},\bar{x})$. The *eigenvector* of a matrix is defined as a non-zero vector that remains unchanged (or at most is scaled by a scalar λ, called *eigenvalue*) when we apply the geometric transformation described by the matrix on it. For example, consider the spinning movement of our planet around its axis. The rotation movement can be mapped into a matrix that, given any point on the globe, can tell where that point will be located after applying a rotation to it. The only points whose locations don't change when the rotation is applied are those along the rotation axis. We can then say that the rotation axis is the *eigenvector* of the matrix associated to the rotation of our planet and that, at least in this specific case, the *eigenvalue* for that vector is $\lambda = 1$—the points along the axis don't change at all during the rotation; they are not even scaled. The case of the rotation of a sphere has a single eigenvector (the rotation axis), but other geometric transformations might have multiple eigenvectors, each with a different associated eigenvalue. To formalize this intuition, we say that, given a matrix $A \in \mathfrak{R}^{n \times n}$ that describes a certain geometric transformation in an n-dimensional space, its eigenvector $\bar{v}$ must be a vector that is at most scaled by a factor λ when we apply A to it:

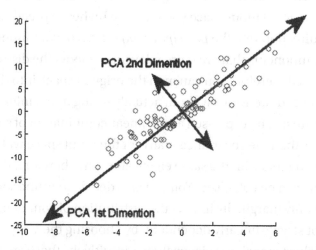

Figure 1-6. *Principal component analysis of a normalized dataset. The vectors in green indicate the components that are more influential in the distribution of the data. You may want to map your input data to this new system of coordinates. You can also select only the largest vector without actually losing a lot of information*

$$A\bar{v} = \lambda\bar{v} \tag{1.27}$$

By grouping $\bar{v}$ in the preceding equation, we get

$$\bar{v}(A - \lambda I_n) = 0 \tag{1.28}$$

where I_n is the *identity matrix* (a matrix with 1s on the main diagonal and 0s everywhere else) of size $n \times n$. The preceding vectorial notation can be expanded into a set of n equations, and by solving them, we can get the eigenvalues λ of A. By replacing the eigenvalues in the preceding equation, we can then get the eigenvectors associated to the matrix.

There is a geometric intuition behind computing the eigenvectors of the auto-covariance matrix. Those eigenvectors indicate in which direction in the n-dimensional input space you have the highest "spread" of the data. Those directions are the *principal components* of your input space, that is, the components that are more relevant to model the distribution of your data, and therefore you can map the original space into the newer space with lower dimensions without actually losing much information. If an input feature can be expressed as the linear combination of some other input features, then the covariance matrix of the input space will have two or more eigenvectors with the same eigenvalue, and therefore, the number of dimensions can be collapsed. You can also decide to prune some features that only marginally impact the distribution of your data, even if they are not strictly linearly dependent, by choosing the k eigenvectors with the k highest associated eigenvalues—intuitively, those are the components that matter the most in the distribution of your data—an example is shown in Figure 1-6.

Once we have the principal components of our input space, we need to transform our input space by reorienting its axes along the eigenvectors— note that those eigenvectors are orthogonal to each other, just like the axes of a Cartesian plane. Let's call W the matrix constructed from the selected principal components (eigenvectors of the auto-covariance matrix). Given a normalized dataset represented by a matrix X, its points will be mapped into the new space through

$$\hat{X} = XW \tag{1.29}$$

We will then train our algorithms on the new matrix $\hat{X}$, whose number of dimensions will be equal or lower than the initial number of features without significant information loss.

Many Python libraries for machine learning and data science already feature some functions for principal component analysis. An example that uses "scikit-learn":

```
import numpy as np

from sklearn.decomposition import PCA

# Input vector

x = np.array([[-1, -1], [-2, -1], [-3, -2], [1, 1], [2, 1],
[3, 2]])

# Define a PCA model that brings the components down to 2

pca = PCA(n_components=2)

# Fit the input data through the model

pca.fit(x)
```

PCA has some obvious advantages—among those, it reduces the dimensionality of an input space with a high number of features analytically, reduces the risk of overfit, and improves the performance of your algorithms. However, it maps the original input space into a new space built out of the principal components, and those new synthetic features may not be intuitive to grasp as real-world features such as "size," "distance," or "time." Also, if you pick a number of components that is lower than the actual number of components that influence your data, you may lose information, so it's a good practice to usually compare the performance of a model before and after applying PCA to check whether you have removed some features that you actually need.

1.5.3 Training set and test set

The first linear regression example we saw was trained on a quite small dataset; therefore, we decided to both train and test the model on the same dataset. In all the real-world scenarios, however, you will usually train your model on very large datasets, and it's important to evaluate your model on data points that your model hasn't been trained on. To do so, the input dataset is conventionally split into two:

1. The **training set** contains the data points your model will be trained on.

2. The **test set** contains the data points your model will be evaluated on.

Figure 1-7. *Example of a 70/30 training set/test set split*

	MPG	Cylinders	Displacement	Horsepower	Weight	Acceleration	Model Year
27.0	4	140.0	86.0	2790.0	15.6	82	1
44.0	4	97.0	52.0	2130.0	24.6	82	2
32.0	4	135.0	84.0	2295.0	11.6	82	1
28.0	4	120.0	79.0	2625.0	18.6	82	1
31.0	4	119.0	82.0	2720.0	19.4	82	1

Figure 1-8. *A look at the Auto MPG dataset*

This is usually done by *splitting* your dataset according to a predefined fraction—the items on the left of the pivot will make the training set, and the ones on the right will make the test set, as shown in Figure 1-7. A few observations on the dataset split:

1. The split fraction you want to choose depends largely on your dataset. If you have a very large dataset (let's say millions of data points or more), then you can select a large training set split (e.g., 90% training set and 10% test set), because even if the fraction of the test set is small, it will still include tens or hundreds of thousands of items, and that will still be significant enough to evaluate your model. In scenarios with smaller dataset, you may want to experiment with different fractions to find the best trade-off between *exploitation* of the available data for training purposes and *statistic significance* of the test set selected to evaluate your model. In other words, you may want to find the trade-off between *exploitation* of the available data for training purposes and *evaluation* of your model on a statistically significant set of data.

2. If your dataset is sorted according to some feature, then make sure to shuffle it before performing the split. It is quite important that the data your model is both trained and evaluated on is as uniform as possible.

1.5.4 Loading and visualizing the dataset

In this example, we will load the Auto MPG dataset [15], a dataset that includes several parameters about 1970s–1980s cars (cylinders, weight, acceleration, year, horsepower, fuel efficiency, etc.). We want to build a model that predicts fuel efficiency of a car from those years given the respective input features.

First, let's download the dataset, load it in our notebook, and take a look at it:

```python
import pandas as pd
import matplotlib.pyplot as plt
dataset_url = 'http://archive.ics.uci.edu/ml/' +
               'machine-learning-databases/' +
               'auto-mpg/auto-mpg.data'
# These are the dataset columns we are interested in
columns = ['MPG','Cylinders','Displacement','Horsepower',
           'Weight', 'Acceleration', 'Model Year']
# Load the CSV file
dataset = pd.read_csv(dataset_url, names=columns,
    na_values = "?", comment='\t',
    sep=" ", skipinitialspace=True)
# The dataset contains some empty cells - remove them
dataset = dataset.dropna()
# Take a look at the last few records of the dataset
dataset.tail()
```

CHAPTER 1   INTRODUCTION TO MACHINE LEARNING

You will probably see a table like the one shown in Figure 1-8. Let's also take a look at how the features correlate to each other. We will use the seaborn library for it and in particular the pairplot method to visualize how each metric's data points plot against each of the other metrics:

```
sns.pairplot(dataset[["MPG", "Cylinders", "Displacement",
"Weight"]], diag_kind="kde")
```

You should see a plot like the one shown in Figure 1-9. Each graph plots the data points broken down by a pair of metrics: that's a useful way to spot correlations. You'll notice that the number of cylinders, displacement, and weight are quite related to MPG, while other metrics are more loosely related against each other.

We will now split the dataset into two, as shown in Section 1.5.3. The training set will contain 80% of the data and the test set the remaining 20%:

```
# Random state initializes the random seed for randomizing
the
# seed. If None then it will be calculated automatically
train_dataset = dataset.sample(frac=0.8, random_state=1)
# The test dataset contains all the records after the split
test_dataset = dataset.drop(train_dataset.index)
# Fuel efficiency (MPG) will be our output label, so drop
# it from the training and test datasets
train_labels = train_dataset.pop('MPG')
test_labels = test_dataset.pop('MPG')
```

And normalize the data:

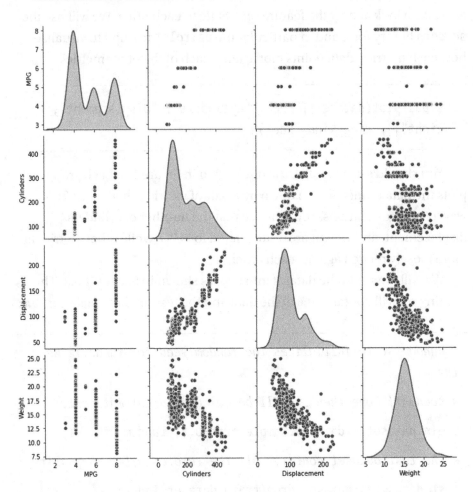

Figure 1-9. *A look at how each feature relates to each other feature through seaborn*

```
def normalize(x, stats):

    return (x - stats['mean']) / stats['std']

def denormalize(x, stats):

    return x * stats['std'] + stats['mean']
```

```
data_stats = train_dataset.describe().transpose()

label_stats = train_labels.describe().transpose()

norm_train_data = normalize(train_dataset, data_stats)

norm_train_labels = normalize(train_labels, label_stats)
```

Then, just like in the previous example, we will define a linear model and try to fit it through our data:

```
from tensorflow.keras.experimental import LinearModel

model = LinearModel(len(train_dataset.keys()),

    activation='linear', dtype='float32')

model.compile(optimizer='rmsprop', loss='mse', metrics=['mae',
'mse'])

history = model.fit(norm_train_data, norm_train_labels,
epochs=200,

    verbose=0)
```

The differences this time are

- The model in the previous example had a single input unit; this one has as many input units as the columns of our training set (excluding the output features).

- We use two evaluation metrics this time, both mae and mse. In most of the cases, it's a good practice to keep a primary evaluation metric other than the loss function.

Let's plot again the loss function over the training iterations:

```
epochs = history.epoch
loss = history.history['loss']
fig = plt.figure()
plot = fig.add_subplot()
plot.set_xlabel('epoch')
plot.set_ylabel('loss')
plot.plot(epochs, loss)
```

You should see a figure like the one shown in Figure 1-10.

Also, we can now evaluate the model on the test set and see how it performs on data it has not been trained on:

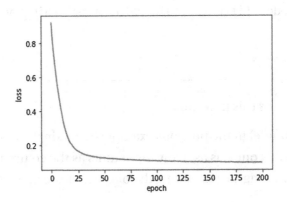

Figure 1-10. *Loss function progress over the multivariate regression training*

```
norm_test_data = normalize(test_dataset, data_stats)

norm_test_labels = normalize(test_labels, label_stats)

model.evaluate(norm_test_data, norm_test_labels)
```

Keep in mind that so far we have been using a single regression unit: things can be even better when we pack many of them into a neural network. We can pick some values from the test set and see how far the model's predictions are from the expected labels:

```
sampled_data = norm_test_data.iloc[:10]

sampled_labels = denormalize(norm_test_labels.iloc[:10],
label_stats)

predictions = [p[0] for p in

    denormalize(model.predict(sampled_data), label_stats)]

for i in range(10):

    print(f'predicted: {predictions[i]} ' +

        f'actual: {sampled_labels.iloc[i]}')
```

Plotting these values on a bar chart should result in a figure like the one shown in Figure 1-11.

You can then perform minimal changes to the model_save and model_load we have encountered in Section 1.4.7 to save and load your model from another notebook or application.

1.6 Polynomial regression

We now know how to create linear regression models on one or multiple input variables. We have seen that these models can be geometrically represented by n-dimensional linear *hyper-surfaces* in the $n + 1$-dimensional space that consists of the n-dimensional input features plus the output feature y—the model will be a line that goes through points in a 2D space in the case of univariate linear regression, it will be a 2D surface that goes through points in a 3D space if you have two input features and one output variable, and so on.

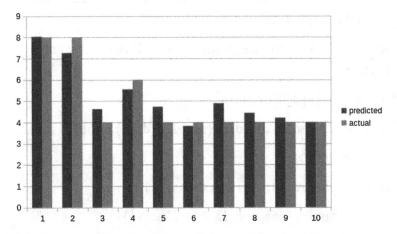

Figure 1-11. *Comparison between the predicted and expected values*

However, not all the problems in the real world can be approximated by linear models. Consider the dataset under `<REPO_DIR>/datasets/house-size-price-2.csv`. It's a variant of the house size vs. price dataset we have encountered earlier, but this time, we hit a plateau between the 100–130 square meters range (e.g., houses of that size or with that particular room configuration don't sell much in the location), and then the price keeps increasing again after 130 square meters. Its representation is shown in Figure 1-12. You can't really capture the grow-and-stop-and-grow sequence like this with a straight line alone. Worse, if you try to fit a straight line through this dataset through the linear procedure we have analyzed earlier, the line could end up being "pulled" down by the points around the plateau in order to minimize the overall mean squared error, ending up with a loss of accuracy also on the remaining points in the dataset.

In cases like this, you may instead want to leverage a *polynomial* model. Keep in mind that linear regression can be modelled, in its simplest form, as $h_\theta(x) = \theta_0 + \theta_1 x$, but nothing prevents us from defining a hypothesis function $h_\theta(x)$ represented by higher powers of the x. For instance, this house size-price non-linear model might not be very well represented by a quadratic function—remember that a parabola first goes up and then down, and you don't really expect house prices to go significantly down when the size increases. However, a cubic model could work just fine—remember that a cubic function on a plane looks like two "half-parabolas" stuck together around an *inflection point*, which is also the point of symmetry of the function. So the hypothesis function for this case could be something like this:

$$h_\theta(x) = \theta_0 + \theta_1 x + \theta_2 x^2 + \theta_3 x^3 \tag{1.30}$$

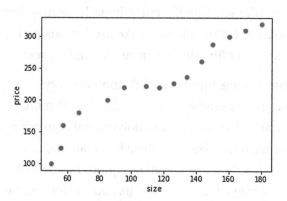

Figure 1-12. *Example of house size vs. price dataset that can't be accurately represented by a linear model*

A clever way to find the values of $\bar{\theta}$ that minimize the preceding function is to treat the additional powers of x as additional variables, perform a variable substitution, and then treat it as a generic multivariate linear regression problem. In other words, we want to translate the problem of gradient descent of a polynomial function into a problem of multivariate linear regression. For instance, we can take the preceding $h_\theta(x)$ expression and rewrite it as a function of $\bar{x}$, where

$$\bar{x} = \left[1, x, x^2, x^3 \right] \tag{1.31}$$

So $h_\theta(x)$ can be rewritten as

$$h_\theta(\bar{x}) = \theta_0 x_0 + \theta_1 x_1 + \theta_2 x_2 + \theta_3 x_3 \tag{1.32}$$

The hypothesis written in this form is the same as the one we have seen in Equation 1.17. We can therefore proceed and calculate the values of θ through the linear multivariate gradient descent procedure we have analyzed, as long as you keep a couple of things in mind:

1. The values of $\bar{\theta}$ that you get out of the algorithm must be plugged into the cubic hypothesis function in Equation 1.30 when you make predictions, not into the linear function we have seen in that section.

2. Feature scaling/input normalization is always important in regression models, but it's even *more* important when it comes to polynomial regression problems. If the size of a house in square meters is in the range $[0, ..., 10^3]$, then its squared value will be in the range $[0, ..., 10^6]$ and its cubic value will be in the range $[0, ..., 10^9]$. If you don't normalize the inputs before feeding them to the model, you will

end up with a model where the highest polynomial terms weigh much more than the rest, and such a model may simply not converge.

3. In the preceding example, we have selected a cubic function because it looks like a good fit for the data at a glance—some growth, an inflection point, and then growth again. However, this won't be true for all the models out there. Some models could perform better with higher polynomial powers (e.g., 4th or 5th powers of the x), or maybe fractional powers of the x—for example, square or cubic roots. Or, in the case of multiple input features, some relations could be well expressed by the product or ratio of some features. The important takeaway here is to *always* look at your dataset before reasoning on what's the best analytical function that can fit it. Sometimes you may also want to try and plot a few sample hypothesis functions to see which one has a shape that best fits your data.

Overall, translating a polynomial regression problem into a multivariate regression problem is a good idea because, as we have seen previously, the cost function of a linear model is usually expressed by a simple n-dimensional quadratic model, which is guaranteed to have only one point with null gradient and that point is also the global minimum. In such configuration, a well-designed gradient descent algorithm should be able to converge toward the optimal solution by simply following the direction of the gradient vector, without getting "stuck" on bumps and valleys that you may get when you differentiate higher polynomial functions.

1.7 Normal equation

Gradient descent is definitely among the most popular approaches for solving regression problems. However, it's not the only way. Gradient descent, as we have seen, finds the parameters $\bar{\theta}$ that optimize the cost function by iteratively "walking" along the direction of the gradient until we hit the minimum. The **normal equation** provides instead an algebraic way to calculate $\bar{\theta}$ in one shot. Such an approach, as we will see soon, has some advantages as well as some drawbacks compared to the gradient descent. In this section, we will briefly cover what the normal equation is and how it is derived, without going too much in depth into the formal proof. I will assume that you have some knowledge of linear algebra and vector/matrix operations (inverse, transpose, and product). If that's not the case, however, feel free to skip this section, or just take note of the final equation. The normal equation provides an analytical alternative to the gradient descent for minimization problems, but it's not strictly required to build models.

We have seen that the generic cost function of a regression model can be written as

$$J(\bar{\theta}) = \frac{1}{2m} \sum_{i=1}^{m} (\bar{\theta}^T \bar{x}_i - y_i)^2 \tag{1.33}$$

And the problem of finding the optimal model is a problem of finding the values of $\bar{\theta}$ such that the gradient vector of $J(\bar{\theta})$ is zero:

$$\nabla J(\bar{\theta}) = \begin{bmatrix} \dfrac{\partial}{\partial \theta_0} J(\bar{\theta}) \\ \vdots \\ \dfrac{\partial}{\partial \theta_n} J(\bar{\theta}) \end{bmatrix} = 0 \tag{1.34}$$

Or, in other words:

$$\frac{\partial}{\partial \theta_j} J(\bar{\theta}) = 0 \text{ for } j = 0, \ldots, n \tag{1.35}$$

If you expand the scalar products and sums in Equation 1.33 for a $X \in \mathfrak{R}^{m \times n}$ dataset, where n is the number of features, m is the number of input samples, and $\bar{y} \in \mathfrak{R}^m$ represents the vector of the output features, and solve the partial derivatives, you get $n + 1$ linear equations, where $\bar{\theta} \in \mathfrak{R}^{n+1}$ represents the variables. Like all systems of linear equations, also this system can be represented as the solution of a matrix $\times$ vector product, and we can solve the associated equation to calculate $\bar{\theta}$. It turns out that $\bar{\theta}$ can be inferred by solving the following equation:

$$\bar{\theta} = \left(X^T X \right)^{-1} X^T \bar{y} \tag{1.36}$$

where X is the $m \times n$ matrix associated to the input features of your dataset (with an added $x_0 = 1$ term at the beginning of each vector, as we have previously seen), X^T denotes the *transposed* matrix (i.e., the matrix you get by swapping rows and columns), the $^{-1}$ operator denotes the *inverse matrix*, and $\bar{y}$ is the vector of output features of your dataset.

The normal equation has a few advantages over the gradient descent algorithm:

1. You won't need to perform several iterations nor risk getting stuck or diverging: the values of $\bar{\theta}$ are calculated straight away by solving the system of $n + 1$ associated gradient linear equations.

2. As a consequence, you won't need to choose a learning rate parameter α, as there's no incremental learning procedure involved.

However, it has a few drawbacks:

1. The gradient descent will still perform well even if the number of input features n is very large. A higher number of feature translates in a larger scalar product in your θ-update steps, and the complexity of a scalar product increases linearly when n grows. On the other hand, a larger value of n means a larger X^TX matrix in Equation 1.36, and calculating the inverse of a very large matrix is a very computationally expensive procedure (it has a $O(n^3)$ complexity). It means that the normal equation could be a good solution for solving regression problems with a low number of input features, while gradient descent will perform better on datasets with more columns.

2. The normal equation works only if the X^TX matrix is *invertible*. A matrix is invertible only if it is a *full rank* square matrix, that is, its rank equals its number of rows/columns, and therefore, it has a non-zero *determinant*. If X^TX is not full rank, it means that either you have some linearly dependent rows or columns (therefore, you have to remove some redundant features or rows) or that you have more features than dataset items (therefore, you have to either remove some features or add some training examples). These normalization steps are also important in gradient descent, but while a non-invertible dataset matrix could result in either a biased or non-optimal model if you apply gradient descent, it will fail on a division by zero if you apply the normal equation. However, most of the modern

frameworks for machine learning also work in
the case of non-invertible matrices, as they use
mathematical tools for the calculation of the *pseudo-inverse* such as the *Moore-Penrose inverse*. Anyway,
even if the math will still work, keep in mind that a
non-invertible characteristic matrix is usually a flag
for linearly dependent metrics that may affect the
performance of your model, so it's usually a good
idea to prune them before calculating the normal
equation.

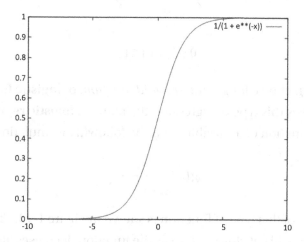

Figure 1-13.   *Plot of the logistic function*

1.8 Logistic regression

Linear regression solves the problem of creating models for numeric
predictions. Not all the problems, however, require predictions in a
numerically continuous domain. We have previously mentioned that
classification problems make up the other large category of problems in
machine learning, that is, problems where instead of a raw numeric value
you want your model to make a prediction about the *class*, or type, of the

provided input (e.g., Is it spam? Is it an anomaly? Does it contain a cat?). Fortunately, we won't need to perform many changes to the regression procedure we have seen so far in order to adapt it to classification problems. We have already learned to define a $h_\theta(\bar{x})$ hypothesis function that maps $\bar{x} \in \Re^n$ to real values. We just need to find a hypothesis function that outputs values such that $0 \le h_\theta(\bar{x}) \le 1$ and define a threshold function that maps the output value to a numeric class (e.g., 0 for *false* and 1 for *true*). In other words, given a linear model $\bar{\theta}^T \bar{x}$, we need to find a function g such that

$$h_\theta(\bar{x}) = g(\bar{\theta}^T \bar{x}) \tag{1.37}$$

$$0 \le h_\theta(\bar{x}) \le 1 \tag{1.38}$$

A common choice for g is the *sigmoid function*, or **logistic function**, which also gives this type of regression the name of **logistic regression**. The logistic function of a variable z has the following formulation:

$$g(z) = \frac{1}{1 + e^{-z}} \tag{1.39}$$

The shape of this type of function is shown in Figure 1-13. The values of the function will get close to zero as the function decreases and close to one as the function increases, and the function has an inflection point around $z = 0$ where its value is 0.5. It is therefore a good candidate to map the outputs of linear regression into the [0...1] range, with a strong non-linearity around the origin to map the "jump." By plugging our linear model into Equation 1.39, we get the formulation of the logistic regression:

$$h_\theta(\bar{x}) = g(\bar{\theta}^T \bar{x}) = \frac{1}{1 + e^{-\bar{\theta}^T \bar{x}}} \tag{1.40}$$

Let's stick for now to the case of logistic regression with a single output class (false/true). We'll see soon how to expand it to multiclass problems as well. If we stick to this definition, then the logistic curve earlier expresses the *probability* for an input to be "true." You can interpret the output value of the logistic function as a *Bayesian* probability—the probability that an item does/does not belong to the output class given its input features:

$$h_\theta(\overline{x}) = P(\text{"true"}|\overline{x}) \tag{1.41}$$

Given the shape of the sigmoid function, we can formalize the classification problem as follows:

$$\text{prediction} = \begin{cases} \text{true if } g(\overline{\theta}^T \overline{x}) \ge 0.5 \\ \text{false if } g(\overline{\theta}^T \overline{x}) < 0.5 \end{cases} \tag{1.42}$$

Since $g(z) \ge 0.5$ when $z \ge 0$, we can reformulate the preceding expression as

$$\text{prediction} = \begin{cases} \text{true if } \overline{\theta}^T \overline{x} \ge 0 \\ \text{false if } \overline{\theta}^T \overline{x} < 0 \end{cases} \tag{1.43}$$

The idea behind logistic regression is to draw a **decision boundary**. If the underlying regression model is a linear model, then imagine drawing a line (or a *hyper-surface*) across your data. The points on the left will represent the negative values and the points on the right the positive values. If the underlying model is a more complex polynomial model, then the decision boundary can be more sophisticated in modelling non-linear relations across the data points.

Let's make an example: consider the dataset under <REPO_DIR>/ datasets/spam-email-1.csv. It contains a dataset for spam email detection, and each row contains the metadata associated to an email.

1. The first row, blacklist_word_count, reports how many words in the email match a blacklist of words often associated to spam emails.

2. The second row, sender_spam_score, is a score between 0 and 1 assigned by a spam filter that represents the probability that the email is spam on the basis of the sender's email address, domain, or internal domain policy.

3. The third row, is_spam, is 0 if the email was not spam and 1 if the email was spam.

We can plot the dataset to see if there is any correlation between the metrics. We will plot blacklist_word_count on the *x* axis and sender_ spam_score on the *y* axis and represent the associated dot in red if it's spam and in blue if it's not spam:

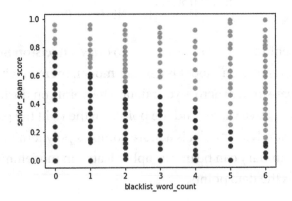

Figure 1-14. *Plot of the spam email dataset*

```python
import pandas as pd
import matplotlib.pyplot as plt
csv_url = 'https://raw.githubusercontent.com/BlackLight' +
          '/mlbook-code/master/datasets/spam-email-1.csv')
data = pd.read_csv(csv_url)
# Split spam and non-spam rows
spam = data[data['is_spam'] == 1]
non_spam = data[data['is_spam'] == 0]
columns = data.keys()
fig = plt.figure()
# Plot the non-spam data points in blue
non_spam_plot = fig.add_subplot()
non_spam_plot.set_xlabel(columns[0])
non_spam_plot.set_ylabel(columns[1])
non_spam_plot.scatter(non_spam[columns[0]], non_
spam[columns[1]], c='b')
# Plot the spam data points in red
spam_plot = fig.add_subplot()
spam_plot.scatter(spam[columns[0]], spam[columns[1]], c='r')
```

You should see a graph like the one shown in Figure 1-14. We can visually see that we can approximately draw a line on the plane to split spam from non-spam. Depending on the slope of the line we pick, we may let a few cases slip through, but a good separation line should be accurate enough to make good predictions in most of the cases. The task of logistic regression is to find the parameters of θ that we can plot in Equation 1.40 to get a good prediction model.

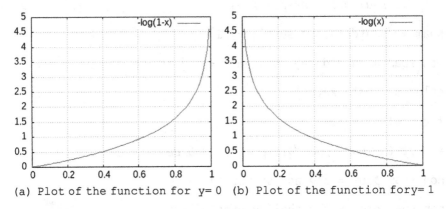

(a) Plot of the function for y= 0   (b) Plot of the function for y= 1

Figure 1-15. *Example plots of the logistic regression cost function* $J(\bar{\theta})$ *with one input variable*

1.8.1 Cost function

Most of the principles we have seen in linear regression (definition of a linear or polynomial model, cost/loss function, gradient descent, feature normalization, etc.) also apply to logistic regression. The main difference consists in how we write the cost function $J(\bar{\theta})$. While the mean squared error is a metric that makes sense when you want to calculate what's the mean error between your prediction of a price and the actual price, it doesn't make much sense when you want to find out if you predicted the correct class of a data point or not, with a given discrete number of classes.

We want to build a cost function that expresses the *classification error*—that is, whether or not the predicted class was correct or wrong—and how "large" the classification error is, that is, how "certain/uncertain" about its classification the model was. Let's rewrite the cost function $J(\bar{\theta})$ we have defined earlier by calling $C(h_\theta(\bar{x}), y)$ its new argument:

$$J(\bar{\theta}) = \frac{1}{m} \sum_{i=1}^{m} C(h_\theta(\bar{x}_i), y_i) \tag{1.44}$$

When it comes to logistic regression, the function C is often expressed in this form (we will stick to a binary classification problem for now, i.e., a problem where there are only two output classes, like *true/false*; we will expand it to multiple classes later):

$$C(h_\theta(\bar{x}), y) = \begin{cases} -\log(h_\theta(\bar{x})) \text{ if } y = 1 \\ -\log(1 - h_\theta(\bar{x})) \text{ if } y = 0 \end{cases} \tag{1.45}$$

The intuition is as follows:

1. If $y_i = 1$ (the class of the i-th data points is positive) and the predicted value $h_\theta(\bar{x})$ also equals 1, then the cost will be zero ($-\log(1) = 0$, i.e., there was no prediction error). The cost will gradually increase as the predicted value gets far from 1. If $y_i = 1$ and $h_\theta(\bar{x}) = 0$, then the cost function will assume an infinite value ($-log(0) = \infty$). In real applications, of course, we won't use infinity, but we may use a very large number instead. The case where the real value is 1 and the predicted value is 0 is like a case where

a model predicts with 100% confidence that it's raining outside while instead it's not raining—if it happens, you want to bring the model back on track by applying a large cost function.

2. Similarly, if $y_i = 0$ and the predicted value also equals 0, then the cost function will be null ($-\log(1 - 0) = 0$).

   If instead $y_i = 0$ and $h_\theta(\overline{x}) = 1$, then the cost will go to infinity.

In the case of one input and one output variable, the plot of the cost function will look like in Figure 1-15. If we combine together the expressions in Equation 1.45, we can rewrite the logistic regression cost function in Equation 1.44 as

$$J\left(\overline{\theta}\right) = -\frac{1}{m}\left[\sum_{i=1}^{m} y^{(i)}\log h_\theta\left(\overline{x}^{(i)}\right) + \left(1 - y^{(i)}\right)\log\left(1 - h_\theta\left(\overline{x}^{(i)}\right)\right)\right] \qquad (1.46)$$

We have compacted together the two expressions of Equation 1.45. If $y_i = 1$, then the first term of the sum in square brackets applies, and if $y_i = 0$, then the second applies.

Just like in linear regression, the problem of finding the optimal values of $\overline{\theta}$ is a problem of minimizing the cost function—that is, perform gradient descent. We can therefore still apply the gradient update steps shown in Equation 1.9 to get the direction to the bottom of the cost function surface. Additionally, just like in linear regression, we are leveraging a *convex* cost function—that is, a cost function with a single null-gradient point that also happens to be the global minimum.

By replacing $h_\theta(\overline{x})$ in the preceding formula with the logistic function defined in Equation 1.40 and solving the partial derivatives in Equation 1.9, we can derive the update step for $\overline{\theta}$ at the $k + 1$-step for logistic regression:

$$\theta_j^{(k+1)} = \theta_j^{(k)} - \frac{\alpha}{m}\sum_{i=1}^{m}\left(h_\theta\left(\overline{x}^{(i)}\right) - y^{(i)}\right)x_j^{(i)} \text{ for } j = 0...n \qquad (1.47)$$

You'll notice that the formulation of the θ-update step is basically the same as we saw for the linear regression in Equation 1.22, even though we've come to it through a different route. And we should have probably expected it, since our problem is still a problem of finding a line that fits our data in some way. The only difference is that the hypothesis function h_θ in the linear case is a linear combination of the $\bar{\theta}$ parameters and the input vector ($\bar{\theta}^T \bar{x}$), while in the logistic regression case, it's the sigmoid function we have introduced in Equation 1.40.

1.8.2 Building the regression model from scratch

We can now extend the gradient descent algorithm we have previously seen for the linear case to work for logistic regression. Let's actually put together all the pieces we have analyzed so far (hypothesis function, cost function, and gradient descent) to build a small framework for regression problems. In most of the cases, you won't have to build a regression algorithm from scratch, but it's a good way to see how the concepts we have covered so far work in practice. First, let's define the hypothesis function for logistic regression:

```python
import math

import numpy as np

def h(theta):
    """

    Return the hypothesis function associated to

    the parameters theta
    """
```

```python
def _model(x):
    """
    Return the hypothesis for an input vector x
    given the parameters theta. Note that we use
    numpy.dot here as a more compact way to
    represent the scalar product theta*x
    """
    ret = 1./(1 + math.exp(-np.dot(theta, x)))
    # Return True if the hypothesis is >= 0.5,
    # otherwise return False
    return ret >= 0.5
return _model
```

Note that if we replace the preceding hypothesis function with the scalar product $\bar{\theta}^T \bar{x}$, we convert a logistic regression problem into a linear regression problem:

```python
import numpy as np
def h(theta):
    def _model(x):
        return np.dot(theta, x)
    return _model
```

Then let's code the gradient descent algorithm:

```python
def gradient_descent(x, y, theta, alpha):
    """

    Perform the gradient descent.
    :param x: Array of input vectors
    :param y: Output vector
    :param theta: Values for theta
    :param alpha: Learning rate
    """

    # Number of samples
    m = len(x)
    # Number of features+1
    n = len(theta)
    new_theta = np.zeros(n)
    # Perform the gradient descent on theta
    for j in range(n):
        for i in range(m):
            new_theta[j] += (h(theta)(x[i]) - y[i]) * x[i][j]
            new_theta[j] = theta[j] - (alpha/m) * new_theta[j]
        return new_theta
```

Then a train method, which consists of *epochs* gradient descent iterations:

```python
def train(x, y, epochs, alpha=0.001):
    """

    Train a model on the specified dataset
    :param x: Array of normalized input vectors
    :param y: Normalized output vector
    :param epochs: Number of training iterations
    :param alpha: Learning rate
    """

    # Set x0=1
    new_x = np.ones((x.shape[0], x.shape[1]+1))
    new_x[:, 1:] = x
    x = new_x
    # Initialize theta randomly
    theta = np.random.randint(low=0, high=10, size=len(x[0]))
    # Perform the gradient descent <epochs> times
    for i in range(epochs):
        theta = gradient_descent(x, y, theta, alpha)
    # Return the hypothesis function associated to
    # the parameters theta
    return h(theta)
```

Finally, a prediction function that, given an input vector, the stats of the dataset, and the model

1. Normalizes the input vector

2. Sets $x_0 = 1$

3. Returns the prediction according to the given hypothesis h_θ

```python
def normalize(x, stats):
    return (x - stats['mean']) / stats['std']
def denormalize(x, stats):
    return stats['std'] * x + stats['mean']
def predict(x, stats, model):
    """

    Make a prediction given a model and an input vector
    """

# Normalize the values
x = normalize(x, stats).values
# Set x0=1
x = np.insert(x, 0, 1.)
# Get the prediction
return model(x)
```

Last, an evaluate function that given a list of input values and the expected outputs evaluates the accuracy (number of correctly classified inputs divided by the total number of inputs) of the given hypothesis function:

```python
def evaluate(x, y, stats, model):
    """

    Evaluate the accuracy of a model.
    :param x: Array of input vectors
    :param y: Vector of expected outputs
    :param stats: Input normalization stats
    :param model: Hypothesis function
    """

    n_samples = len(x)
    ok_samples = 0
    for i, row in x.iterrows():
        expected = y[i]
        predicted = predict(row, stats, model)
        if expected == predicted:
            ok_samples += 1
    return ok_samples/n_samples
```

Now, let's give this framework a try by training and evaluating a model for spam detection on the dataset that we have previously loaded:

```
columns = dataset_stats.keys()
# x contains the input features (first two columns)
inputs = data.loc[:, columns[:2]]
# y contains the output features (last column)
outputs = data.loc[:, columns[2]]
# Get the statistics for inputs and outputs
x_stats = inputs.describe().transpose()
y_stats = outputs.describe().transpose()
# Normalize the features
norm_x = normalize(inputs, x_stats)
norm_y = normalize(outputs, y_stats)
# Train a classifier on the normalized data
spam_classifier = train(norm_x, norm_y, epochs=100)
# Evaluate the accuracy of the classifier
accuracy = evaluate(inputs, outputs, x_stats, spam_classifier)
print(accuracy)
```

Hopefully you should measure a >85% accuracy, which isn't that bad if we look back at how the original data is distributed, and the fact that we defined a linear decision boundary.

1.8.3 The TensorFlow way

Now that we have learned all the nuts and bolts of a regression model, let's build a logistic regression model to solve our spam classification problem with TensorFlow. Only few tweaks are required to the example we have previously seen for linear regression:

```python
from tensorflow.keras.experimental import LinearModel

columns = dataset_stats.keys()

# Input features are on the first two columns

inputs = data.loc[:, columns[:2]]

# Output feature is on the last column

outputs = data.loc[:, columns[2:]]

# Normalize the inputs

x_stats = inputs.describe().transpose()

norm_x = normalize(inputs, x_stats)

# Define and compile the model

model = LinearModel(2, activation='sigmoid', dtype='float32')

model.compile(optimizer='sgd', loss='sparse_categorical_
crossentropy',

    metrics=['accuracy', 'sparse_categorical_crossentropy'])

# Train the model

history = model.fit(norm_x, outputs, epochs=700, verbose=0)
```

A few changes in the preceding code compared to the linear model:

- We use the sigmoid activation function, as defined in Equation 1.39, instead of linear.

- We use the sgd optimizer—*stochastic gradient descent.*

- We use a categorical cross-entropy loss function, similar to the one defined in Equation 1.46.

- We use accuracy (i.e., number of correctly classified samples divided by the total number of samples) as a performance metric.

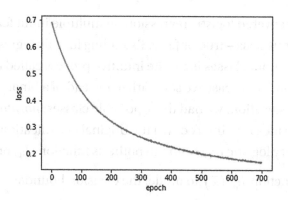

Figure 1-16. *Loss function of the logistic model over training epochs*

Let's see how the loss function progressed over the training iterations:

```
epochs = history.epoch

loss = history.history['loss']

fig = plt.figure()

plot = fig.add_subplot()
```

```
plot.set_xlabel('epoch')
plot.set_ylabel('loss')

plot.plot(epochs, loss)
```

You should see a graph like the one shown in Figure 1-16.

All the other model methods we saw for the linear regression case—evaluate, predict, save, and load—will also work for the logistic regression case.

1.8.4 Multiclass regression

We have so far covered logistic regression on multiple input features but one single output class—true or false. Extending logistic regression to work with multiple output classes is a quite intuitive process called *one vs. all*.

Suppose that in the case we saw earlier, instead of a binary spam/non-spam classification, we had three possible classes: *normal, important,* and *spam*. The idea is to break down the original classification problem into three binary logistic regression hypothesis functions h_θ, one per class:

1. A function $h_\theta^{(1)}(\bar{x})$ to model the decision boundary *normal/not normal*

2. A function $h_\theta^{(2)}(\bar{x})$ to model the decision boundary *important/not important*

3. A function $h_\theta^{(3)}(\bar{x})$ to model the decision boundary *spam/not spam*

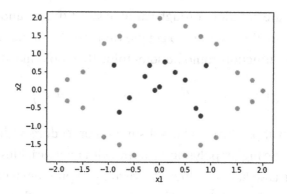

Figure 1-17. *Plot of a dataset with a non-linear decision boundary*

Each hypothesis function represents the probability that an input vector belongs to a specific class. Therefore, the hypothesis function with the highest value is the one the input belongs to. In other words, given an input $\bar{x}$ and c classes, we want to pick the class for $\bar{x}$ that has the highest hypothesis function value associated:

$$\max_{0 \leq i \leq c} h_\theta^{(i)}(\bar{x}) \tag{1.48}$$

The intuition is that the hypothesis function with the highest value represents the class with the highest probability, and that's the prediction we want to pick.

1.8.5 Non-linear boundaries

So far we have explored logistic regression models where the argument of the sigmoid is a linear function. However, just like in linear regression, not all the classification problems out there can be modelled by drawing linear decision boundaries. The distribution of the dataset in Figure 1-17 is definitely not well fit for a linear decision boundary, but an elliptic decision boundary could do the job quite well. Just like we saw in linear regression, a non-linear model function can effectively be translated into a linear multivariate function through variable substitution, and we can then minimize that function in order to get the values of $\bar{\theta}$. In the case earlier, a good hypothesis function could be something that looks like this:

$$h_\theta\left(\bar{x}\right) = g\left(\theta_0 x_0 + \theta_1 x_1 + \theta_2 x_2 + \theta_3 x_1 x_2 + \theta_4 x_1^2 + \theta_5 x_2^2\right) \qquad (1.49)$$

We can then apply the variable substitution procedure we have already seen to replace the higher polynomial terms with new variables and proceed with solving the associated multivariate regression problem with a linear model to get the values of $\bar{\theta}$. Just like in linear regression, there is no limit to the number of additional polynomial terms you can add to your model to better express complex decision boundaries—take into account anyway that adding too many polynomial terms could end up modelling decision boundaries that may overfit your data. As we will see later, another common approach for detecting non-linear boundaries is to connect multiple logistic regression units together—that is, building a *neural network*.

CHAPTER 2

Neural Networks

Now that we have an idea of how to use regression to train a model, it's time to explore the next step—fitting multiple regression units into a neural network.

Neural networks come as a better approach to solve complex regression or classification problems with non-linear dependencies between the input features. We have seen that linear regression and logistic regression with linear functions can perform well if the features of the underlying data are bound by linear relations. In that case, fitting a line (or a linear hyper-surface) through your data is a good strategy to train a model. We have also seen that more complex non-linear relations can be expressed by adding more polynomial terms to the hypothesis function—for instance, quadratic or cubic relations or terms with the product of some features.

There's a limit, however, to adding more synthetic features as extra polynomial terms. Consider the example shown in Figure 2-1. A linear division boundary may not be that accurate in describing the relation between the input features. We can add more polynomial terms (e.g., $x_1 x_2$, x_1^2, or $x_1 x_2^2$), and that could indeed fit our data well, but we're running the risk of overfitting the dataset (i.e., produce a model that performs well on the specific training input but is not generic enough for other cases). Moreover, the approach may still be sustainable if we only have two input features. Try, however, to picture a real-case scenario like the price of a house, which can depend on a vast amount of features that are not

© Fabio Manganiello 2021
F. Manganiello, *Computer Vision with Maker Tech*,
https://doi.org/10.1007/978-1-4842-6821-6_2

necessarily linearly related, and you'll notice that the number of additional polynomial features required by your model will easily explode. Training a regression model with multiple input features and multiple non-linear terms has two big drawbacks:

- The relations between the features are hard to visualize.

- It's an approach prone to the combinational explosion. You'll be likely to end up with a lot of features to express all the relations. Such a model will be very expensive to train while still prone to overfit.

And things only get trickier when we move to the domain of image detection. Keep in mind that a computer only sees the raw pixel values in an image, and objects that are pictured in an image often have non-linear boundaries.

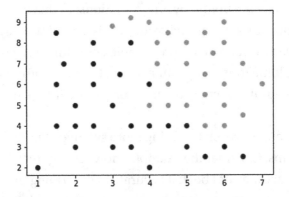

Figure 2-1. *Example of non-linear boundary between two variables that can be tricky to express with logistic regression alone*

When your data consists of many input features and when the distribution of your data or the boundaries between its classes are non-linear, it's usually a better idea to organize your regression classifiers into a network to better capture the increased complexity, instead of attempting to build a single regression classifier that maybe comes with a lot of polynomial terms to best describe your training set but can easily end up overfitting your data without actually providing good predictions. The idea is similar to the way most of the animals (and humans) learn. The neurons in our system are strongly wired together through a structure akin to the one shown in Figure 2-2, and they continuously interact through small variations of electric potential both with the periphery of the body (on fibers called *axons*, each connected to a neuron, if you bundle more axons together you get a *nerve*) and with other neurons (on connection fibers called *dendrites*). The connections between the axon from a neuron and the dendrites of the next neuron are called *synapses*. The electrochemical signals sent over these connections are what allows animals to see, hear, smell, or feel pain and what allows us to consciously move an arm or a leg. These connections, however, constantly mutate over a lifetime span. Connections between neurons are forged on the basis of the sensory signals that are gathered from the environment around and on the basis of the experience we collect. We don't innately know how to grasp an object the right way, but we gradually learn it within the first months of our lives. We don't innately know how to speak the language of our parents, but we gradually learn it as we are exposed to more and more examples. Physically, this happens by a continuous process of fine-tuning of the connections between neurons in order to optimize how we perform a certain task. Neurons quickly specialize to perform a certain task—those in the back of our head process the images from our eyes, while those in the pre-frontal cortex are usually in charge for abstract thought and planning—by synchronizing with their connected neighbors. Neurons quickly learn to fire electrochemical impulses or stay silent whenever the net input signals are above or below a certain threshold, and connections are continuously re-modelled, according to the idea that neurons that fire together wire together more strongly. And the nervous system is in charge not only of creating new connections to better react to the environment but also to keep the number of connections optimized—if each neuron was strongly connected to all other neurons, our bodies would require a lot of energy just to keep all the connections running—so neural paths that aren't used for a certain period of time eventually lose their strength; that's why, for example, we tend to forget notions that we haven't refreshed for a long time.

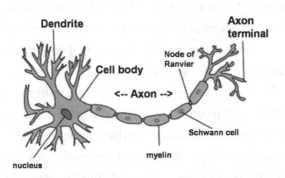

Figure 2-2. *Principal components of a physical neuron*

Artificial neural networks are modelled in a way that closely mimics their biological counterparts. Not only that, but the fields of artificial intelligence and neuroscience have a longstanding tradition of influencing each other—artificial neural networks are modelled mimicking the biological networks, while progress in the development of artificial neural networks often sheds light on overlooked features of the brain. Imagine each neuron in an artificial neural network as a computational unit with a certain number of inputs, which approximately map the dendrites in the physical cell. Each input "wire" has a *weight* that can be adjusted during the learning phase, which approximately maps the synapses of the physical neuron. The neuron itself can be seen as a computational unit that performs the *weighted sum* of its inputs and applies a non-linear function (like the logistic curve we have previously seen) to map an on/off output state. If the output of the activation function is higher than a certain threshold, then the neuron will "fire" a signal. The output of each neuron can either be fed to another neuron or be one of the terminal outputs of your network. The simplest case of a network is the *perceptron* (see

Figure 2-3), similar to what Frank Rosenblatt designed in 1957 to try and recognize people in images. It's a network with a single neuron with a set of $n + 1$ input features $\bar{x} = [x_0, x_1, x_2, ..., x_n]$ (just like in the case of regression, we are using an accessory $x_0 = 1$ input to express the linear model in a more compact way). Each of the inputs is connected to a neuron through a vector of $n + 1$ weights $theta = [\theta_0, \theta_1, \theta_2, ..., \theta_n]$. The unit will output an *activation value* $a(\bar{x})$, defined as the weighted sum of its inputs:

$$a(\bar{x}) = \sum_{i=0}^{n} \theta_i x_i \tag{2.1}$$

Such activation value will go through an *activation function* $h_\theta(x)$, usually the sigmoid/logistic function we saw in Equation 1.39, that will map the real value onto a discrete on/off value:

$$g(z) = \frac{1}{1 + e^{-z}} \tag{2.2}$$

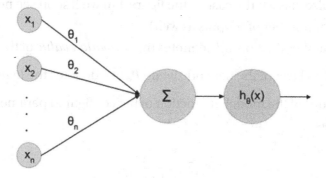

Figure 2-3. *Logic model of a network with a single neuron (perceptron)*

Such a learning unit can work for some simple cases, but in more complex cases, it will face the same issues encountered by Rosenblatt's first perceptron. Spotting people or objects in images is a learning problem with a high number of inputs—in its most naive implementation, each pixel of the image will be an input of the model. A single neuron isn't sufficient in general to model such a high level of variability. That's why nowadays it's much more common to pack multiple perceptron units into a *neural network*, where each output of each neuron is connected to the input of the neuron in the next layer, as shown in Figure 2-4. By packing more interconnected neurons, a learning unit usually becomes better at recognizing complex patterns in problems with a high number of dimensions. The example in the figure shows a neural network with three layers. This is a quite common architecture for simple cases, but we'll soon see that problems with more nuanced patterns can better be solved with networks with more intermediate layers. By convention, the first layer is called *input layer*, and it usually has as many neurons as the dimensions of the input datasets (plus one, with $x_0 = 1$). The second and any other intermediate layer is usually called *hidden layer*, as they do most of the inference work, but they are not directly connected neither to the inputs nor to the outputs of the network. The last layer of the network is called *output layer*, and it contains as many outputs as the output classes/labels (one true/false class in the case in the figure, but we'll soon see network with a higher number of outputs as well).

Note that the notation $a_i^{(j)}$ denotes the *activation value* of the i-th unit in the j-th layer of the network, while $h_\Theta(\bar{x})$ denotes the *hypothesis* (or prediction) of the model in function of the configured parameters Θ, calculated as

$$h_\Theta(\bar{x}) = \frac{1}{1 + e^{-\Theta\bar{x}}}$$

While in the regression case the parameters (or weights) of the model were a vector, in this case, each j-th layer will have an associated $\Theta^{(j)}$ matrix to map the weights between the j-th and the $j + 1$-th layer. Remember that each of the units in j is connected to each of the units in $j + 1$, so Θ_j will be a $m \times n$ matrix, where m is the number of units in j and n is the number of units in $j + 1$. Therefore, we can visualize Θ as a 3D *tensor*. Intuitively, a tensor is a multi-dimensional generalization of a matrix. In our case, each j-th "slice" of the tensor Θ represents the 2D matrix of weights of the j-th layer.

If we put together all the pieces of information we've gathered so far, we can formalize the activation function of each neuron in the figure as follows:

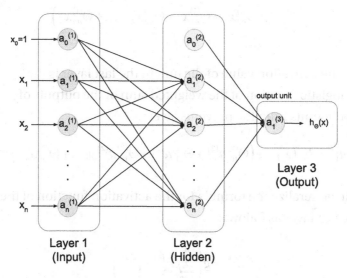

Figure 2-4. *Logic model of an artificial neural network with three layers*

- The units in the first layer are usually mapped one-to-one to the input features, unless you want to assign each feature a different weight:

$$a_i^{(1)} = x_i \text{ for } i = 0 \ldots n$$

- The activation values of the units in the second layer is the logistic function of the weighted sum of the inputs:

$$a_1^{(2)} = g\left(\Theta_{10}^{(1)}x_0 + \Theta_{11}^{(1)}x_1 + \Theta_{12}^{(1)}x_2 + \ldots + \Theta_{1n}^{(1)}x_n\right)$$

$$a_2^{(2)} = g\left(\Theta_{20}^{(1)}x_0 + \Theta_{21}^{(1)}x_1 + \Theta_{22}^{(1)}x_2 + \ldots + \Theta_{2n}^{(1)}x_n\right)$$

$$\ldots$$

$$a_n^{(2)} = g\left(\Theta_{n0}^{(1)}x_0 + \Theta_{n1}^{(1)}x_1 + \Theta_{n2}^{(1)}x_2 + \ldots + \Theta_{nn}^{(1)}x_n\right)$$

- The activation value of the unit in the last layer is the logistic function of the weighted sum of the outputs of the units from the previous layer:

$$a_1^{(3)} = h_\Theta(\overline{x}) = g\left(\Theta_{10}^{(2)}a_0^{(2)} + \Theta_{11}^{(2)}a_1^{(2)} + \Theta_{12}^{(2)}a_2^{(2)} + \ldots + \Theta_{1n}^{(2)}a_n^{(2)}\right)$$

We can generalize the formula for the activation function of the i-th unit in the j-th layer as follows:

$$a_i^{(j)} = g\left(\sum_{k=0}^{n}\Theta_{ik}^{(j-1)}a_k^{(j-1)}\right) \tag{2.3}$$

Or, using a vectorial notation, we can describe the vector of activation values of the units in the j-th layer as

$$\overline{a}^{(j)} = g\left(\Theta^{(j-1)^T}\overline{a}^{(j-1)}\right) \tag{2.4}$$

Such algorithm is commonly known as **forward-propagation**, and it's how a neural network with a certain set of weights makes predictions given some input data—the intuition is basically to *propagate* the input values through each node, from input to output layer. Forward-propagation can be seen as a generalization of the hypothesis function used in logistic regression in a multi-unit scenario. A couple of observations:

- Keep in mind that g is the logistic function, and we use it on each layer to "discretize" the weighted sum of the inputs.

- We have so far set $x_0 = 1$, so that each of the input vectors actually has size $n + 1$. We keep this practice also for neural networks, each j-th layer will have its own *bias unit* $a_0^{(j)}$. We can assume that these bias values always equal one for now, but we will see later on how to tune the bias vector to improve the performance of our models.

- In the example we've considered so far both the input and hidden layer have $n + 1$ units. While the input layer has indeed $n + 1$ units in most of the cases, where n is the dimension of the inputs, and the output layer mostly has as many units as the number of output classes, there is no constraint on the number of units in the hidden layer. Actually, it's a common practice in many cases to have more units (at least in the first hidden layer) than the number of the input dimensions, but keep an eye on the performance of your model to make sure that you don't keep adding hidden units beyond a point that doesn't actually improve your performance metrics.

- As I mentioned earlier, there's no constraint on the number of hidden layers either. Indeed, adding more hidden layers will usually improve the performance of your model in many cases, as your network will be able to detect more nuanced patterns. However, just like the good practice for the number of units, you may also not want to overengineer your model by adding more layers than those actually required by the type of classification problems you want to solve, since adding either too many intermediate layers or units may have no measurable impact on the network in the best case and deteriorate the performance of the network because of overfit in the worst case. Again, the best practice is to try different number of layers with different number of units and see when you hit the "sweet spot" between good model performance metrics and good system performance metrics.

2.1 Back-propagation

If forward-propagation is the way a neural network makes predictions, back-propagation is the way a neural network "learns"—that is, how it adjusts its tensor of weights Θ given a training set. Just like we did for regression, also for neural networks, the learning phase can be inferred by defining a *cost function* that we want to optimize.

In the general case, you will have a neural network with K outputs, where those outputs are the classes that you want to detect. Each output expresses the *probability*, between 0 and 1, that a certain input belongs to that class. If the input of your network are pictures of items of clothing, for example, and you want to detect whether a picture contains a shirt, a skirt, or a pair of trousers, you may want to model a neural network with three output units. If a picture contains a shirt, for instance, you want that network to output something close to $[1, 0, 0]$. If it's a pair of trousers, you want it to output something like $[0, 0, 1]$, and so on. So instead of a hypothesis function with a single output variable, like we have seen so far, you will have a hypothesis functions $h_\Theta(\bar{x}) \in \mathfrak{R}^K$ with a vector of K values, one for each class. The prediction class of your model will usually be the index of the $h_\Theta(\bar{x})$ function with the highest value:

$$\text{class} = \text{argmax}_i h_\Theta^{(i)}(\bar{x})$$

In the previous example, if you get a hypothesis vector like $[0.8, 0.2, 0.1]$ for a certain picture, and your output units are set in the order $[shirt, skirt, trousers]$, then it's likely that that picture contains a shirt.

So the job of the cost function of a neural network is to minimize the classification error between the i-th vector of labels in the training set, $\bar{y}^{(i)}$, and the predicted output vector $h_\Theta(\bar{x})$. We have seen this type of cost function already in the case of a true/false binary classification problem in Equation 1.46, when we covered logistic regression:

$$J(\bar{\theta}) = -\frac{1}{m}\left[\sum_{i=1}^{m} y^{(i)} \log h_\theta\left(\bar{x}^{(i)}\right) + \left(1 - y^{(i)}\right)\log\left(1 - h_\theta\left(\bar{x}^{(i)}\right)\right)\right] \qquad (2.5)$$

If instead of one single label $y^{(i)}$ for the i-th input sample we have a vector of K items, and instead of a one-dimensional vector of weights θ we have a 3D tensor of weights Θ, with each slice representing the weight matrix to map one layer to the next, then the cost function can be rewritten as follows:

$$J(\Theta) = -\frac{1}{m}\left[\sum_{i=1}^{m}\sum_{k=1}^{K}y_k^{(i)}\log\left(h_\Theta\left(\overline{x}^{(i)}\right)\right)_k + \left(1-y_k^{(i)}\right)\log\left(1-h_\Theta\left(\overline{x}^{(i)}\right)\right)_k\right] +$$

$$+\frac{\lambda}{2m}\sum_{l=1}^{L-1}\sum_{i=1}^{s_l}\sum_{j=1}^{s_{l+1}}\left(\Theta_{ij}^{(l)}\right)^2 \tag{2.6}$$

The second term in the sum (multiplied by $\frac{\lambda}{2m}$) is the conventional way to encode the *bias inputs* of each layer (the weights of the $x_0^{(j)}$ elements)—as the sum of the squares of the weights between the l-th and $l+1$-th layer. λ is the *bias rate*, or *regularization rate* of the network, and it defines the *inertia* of the network against changes—a high value in this case leads to a more *conservative* model, that is, a model that will be slower to apply corrections to its weights, while a low value leads to a model that will adapt faster to changes, at the risk of *overfitting* the data. Training phases usually start with a lower bias rate in order to quickly adjust to corrections at the beginning which slowly decreases over time.

Just like in the case of regression, finding the optimal values of Θ is a problem of minimizing the preceding cost function; therefore, perform some form of gradient descent to find its minimum. In neural networks, this process is usually done layer by layer, starting from the output layer and adjusting the weights backward layer by layer (that's why it's called *back-propagation*). The intuition is to first compare the outputs of the network against the expected samples, and as we adjust the weights of the units in the output layer to match the output more closely, we calculate new intermediate expected results for the units in the previous layer, and we proceed with adjusting the weights until we get to the first layer.

Let's consider a network with $L = 4$ layers and two outputs like the one shown in Figure 2-5. If we present it with an input $\overline{x} = [x_1, x_2, x_3]$ and a vector of expected labels $\overline{y} = [y_1, y_2]$ and apply forward-propagation to it, we can calculate its hypothesis function $h_\Theta\left(\overline{x}^{(i)}\right) \in \mathfrak{R}^2$:

$$\overline{a}^{(1)} = \overline{x}$$

$$\overline{a}^{(2)} = g\left(\Theta^{(1)^T} \overline{a}^1\right)$$

$$\overline{a}^{(3)} = g\left(\Theta^{(2)^T} \overline{a}^2\right)$$

$$\overline{a}^{(4)} = h_\Theta\left(\overline{x}\right) = g\left(\Theta^{(3)^T} \overline{a}^3\right)$$

Then, just like in the case of regression, we want to find the values of Θ (which is a 3D tensor in this case) that minimize the cost function $J(\Theta)$. In other words, for each layer l, we want to calculate its gradient vector $\nabla J(\Theta^{(l)})$. We want the values of this vector to be as close as possible to zero:

$$\nabla J\left(\Theta^{(l)}\right)\underset{\text{set}}{=}0 \ \ \forall 1 \leq l \leq L-1$$

It means that the partial derivatives of $J(\Theta^{(l)})$ with respect to its weights $\Theta_{ij}^{(l)}$ should be set to zero, so we can derive the optimal weights out of the resulting equations:

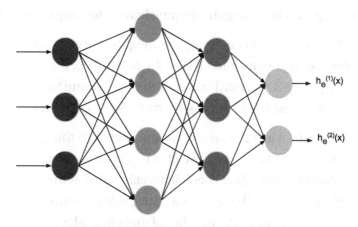

Figure 2-5. *Example of a neural network with L = 4 layers, n = 3 inputs, and K = 2 outputs*

99

$$\frac{\partial}{\partial \Theta_{ij}^{(l)}} J\left(\Theta^{(l)}\right)\Big|_{\text{set}} = 0 \quad \begin{array}{c} 1 \le i \le s_l, \\ 1 \le j \le s_{l+1} \end{array}$$

We then define a quantity $\delta_j^{(l)}$ as the error coefficient of the j-th unit in the l-th layer, starting from the last layer, where the coefficient is defined as

$$\delta_j^{(4)} = a_j^{(4)} - y_j \text{ for } j = 1,2$$

Or, in vectorial form:

$$\bar{\delta}^{(4)} = \bar{a}^{(4)} - \bar{y}$$

Taking into account the error on the output layer, we calculate the correction to the weights that connect those units to the units in the previous layers in the following way:

$$\bar{\delta}^{(3)} = \Theta^{(3)^T} \bar{\delta}^{(4)} \odot \nabla g(\Theta^{(2)^T} \bar{a}^{(2)})$$
$$\bar{\delta}^{(2)} = \Theta^{(2)^T} \bar{\delta}^{(3)} \odot \nabla g(\Theta^{(1)^T} \bar{a}^{(1)})$$

There are quite a few things happening here so let's dig term by term:

- $\Theta^{(3)}$ is the matrix containing the weights that connect the second to the third layer of the network. If, like in Figure 2-5, the third layer has three units and the second layer has four units, then $\Theta^{(3)}$ is a 3×4 matrix.

- We perform a matrix-vector product between the transposed matrix of the weights in a layer and the vector of δ correction coefficients calculated at the following layer. The result is a vector that contains as many elements as the number of units in the layer.

- We then perform an element-wise product (or *Hadamard product*, denoted by ⊙) between that vector and the vector of partial derivatives of the activation function of the units in the layer (using the notation we have seen in Equation 2.4). The element-wise product is intuitively the element-by-element product between two vectors with the same size, for example:

$$\begin{bmatrix} 2 \\ 3 \end{bmatrix} \odot \begin{bmatrix} 4 \\ 5 \end{bmatrix} = \begin{bmatrix} 8 \\ 15 \end{bmatrix}$$

- ∇g is the gradient vector of the activation function (usually the sigmoid function) calculated for each unit.

We can generalize the preceding expression to express the correction coefficients for the units in the *l*-th layer as

$$\bar{\delta}^{(l)} = \Theta^{(l)^T} \bar{\delta}^{(l+1)} \odot \nabla g\left(\Theta^{(l-1)^T} \bar{a}^{(l-1)}\right)$$

The activation function $g\left(\Theta^{(l-1)^T} a^{(l-1)}\right)$, as seen in Equation 2.4, expresses the activation values of the units in the *l*-th layer, $a^{(l)}$. By solving the derivatives, we can infer this formulation for $\delta^{(l)}$:

$$\bar{\delta}^{(l)} = \Theta^{(l)^T} \bar{\delta}^{(l+1)} \odot \bar{a}^{(l)} \odot \left(1 - \bar{a}^{(l)}\right) \tag{2.7}$$

It is possible to prove (although the process of derivation is quite lengthy and we'll skip it in this chapter) that the following relation exists between the partial derivatives of the cost function and the coefficients $\bar{\delta}$ (ignoring for now the bias coefficients and the normalization rate λ):

$$\frac{\partial}{\partial \Theta_{ij}^{(l)}} J(\Theta) = \bar{a}_j^{(l)} \bar{\delta}_i^{(l+1)} \tag{2.8}$$

Since the partial derivatives of the cost function are exactly what we want to minimize, we can use the findings of Equations 2.7 and 2.8 to define how a network with L layers "learns" through cycles of forward and back-propagation on a training set:

- Initialize the weights Θ in your model, either randomly or according to some heuristic, and initialize a tensor Δ that contains the partial derivatives of the cost function for each weight, with $\Delta_{ij}^{(l)} = 0$ for each connection of the i-th unit in the $l + 1$-th layer with the j-th unit in the l-th layer.

- Iterate over all the items in a normalized training set

$$X = \left\{ \left(\overline{x}^{(1)}, \overline{y}^{(1)} \right), \ldots, \left(\overline{x}^{(m)}, \overline{y}^{(m)} \right) \right\}.$$

- For each i-th training item, set $\overline{a}^{(1)} = \overline{x}^{(i)}$ —the input units of the network will be initialized with each of the normalized input vectors.

- Perform forward-propagation to compute the activation values of the units in the next layers, $\overline{a}^{(l)}$, with $1 < l \leq L$:

$$\overline{a}^{(l)} = g\left(\Theta^{(l-1)^T} \overline{a}^{(l-1)} \right)$$

- Set $h_\Theta\left(\overline{x}^{(i)} \right) = \overline{a}^{(L)}$ —the prediction of your network equals the activation values of the units in the last layer.

- Start applying back-propagation by computing the δ vector for the last layer, as the difference between the predicted and expected values:

$$\overline{\delta}^{(L)} = \overline{a}^{(L)} - \overline{y}^{(i)}$$

- Continue back-propagation by computing the δ vectors for the other layers, starting from the $L - 1$-th layer and moving all the way back until the input layer:

$$\bar{\delta}^{(l)} = \Theta^{(l)^T} \bar{\delta}^{(l+1)} \odot \bar{a}^{(l)} \odot \left(1 - \bar{a}^{(l)}\right)$$

- Update the tensor of the corrections to be applied to the weights:

$$\Delta_{ij}^{(l)} \underset{\text{set}}{=} \Delta_{ij}^{(l)} + \bar{a}_j^{(l)} \bar{\delta}_i^{(l+1)}$$

- After iterating on the training set, we will have our tensor Δ fully calculated. We can now take regularization into account by introducing for each layer the bias unit ($j = 0$) and dividing each of the partial derivatives by the number of samples in the training set:

$$\Delta_{ij}^{(l)} \underset{\text{set}}{=} \begin{cases} \dfrac{1}{m} \Delta_{ij}^{(l)} & \text{if } j = 0 \\ \dfrac{1}{m} \Delta_{ij}^{(l)} + \lambda \Theta_{ij}^{(l)} & \text{if } j \neq 0 \end{cases}$$

- We know that

$$\Delta_{ij}^{(l)} = \frac{\partial}{\partial \Theta_{ij}^{(l)}} J(\Theta)$$

- We can therefore plug these values into a gradient descent logic and use a learning rate α to update each weight according to these quantities:

$$\theta_{ij}^{(l)} \underset{\text{set}}{=} \theta_{ij}^{(l)} - \alpha \Delta_{ij}^{(l)}$$

- Apply this algorithm for a given number of *epochs* on your training set or until some convergence criteria are satisfied, and you've got all the ingredients to train a network.

2.2 Implementation guidelines

There are a few good practices that you may want to follow in order to optimize the performance of a neural network:

- *Randomly initialize the weights of the network.* In most of the cases, a random initialization of the weights within a preset interval $[-\epsilon, \epsilon]$ is the best way to initialize your network. If you initialize the weights with zeros (or any other constant), you'll have predictable output values on the first iterations. A random initialization breaks this symmetry, and it's more likely to point your model in the right direction if you train it multiple times than a solution that always initializes the weights in the same way.

- *Perform a gradient check of your model before or during the training phase.* Unlike the cost functions that we have seen in the case of linear and logistic regression, the cost function of a neural network isn't guaranteed to be convex. It means that it's not guaranteed that the model converges on the global minimum if you follow the direction of the gradient vector from any point, because you are no longer rolling a ball down a bowl-shaped hill. It means that you may want to check both that (1) the initial direction you picked for the gradient descent actually leads to a noticeable reduction of the cost function (i.e., you are not stuck in a local valley) and (2) the learning rate is well calibrated—if it's too low, you may be going down too slowly, and if it's too high, the model may overshoot the minimum and not converge at all.

- *Experiment with the architecture of your network.* There's no deterministic rule about how many layers and how many units are the best for solving a certain problem. A general rule of thumb suggests that networks with more intermediate layers and more units in these layers usually perform better. However, you may want to avoid overengineering as well: a simple network to recognize handwritten digits in 8x8 pixel images doesn't necessarily need 10 intermediate layers with hundreds of units each. Not only that, but after a certain point adding more units or layers results in overfitting. So experiment different architectures, see how increasing the number of units or layers affects the performance of your model on the same training set and number of training iterations, and pick an optimal point just before the boost in performance given by a larger network is negligible.

- *Always normalize your input data before feeding the network.* I've already stressed this enough when it comes to regression, and it's also important in neural networks.

2.2.1 Underfit and overfit

There is always a healthy balance to seek when you train any model between high bias/low variance (or *underfit*) and high variance/low bias (or *overfit*). We have seen these issues already when we covered regression models, and we have discovered the importance of plotting your normalized dataset to get an idea of how the data is distributed before picking a function that has either fewer polynomial terms (*underfit*, the line/surface of the model is too "smooth" and doesn't really follow the distribution of the data) or too many (*overfit*, the line/surface of the model follows exactly the distribution of the data but fails in accuracy when provided with any data point that doesn't look like those it was trained on). These observations also apply when it comes to neural networks. The best way to evaluate the performance of your network against underfit/overfit is, again, to split your dataset into two—training set and test set. Train your network on the training set and evaluate how the cost function progress over the training iterations:

- If the cost function doesn't decrease (or, worse, increases, or goes through up/down cycles), then the model is not converging toward a minimum: make sure that the data is normalized, revise your gradient descent strategy, or reduce the learning rate α.

- If the cost function decreases too slowly, then it's not fast enough at adapting to the changes presented in the training set: you may want to either increase the learning rate α, decrease the normalization rate λ, or add more features to your data.

- If the cost function decreases in a satisfying way and your model seems to make accurate predictions on the training set, then evaluate it on the test set (this time without training: only perform forward-propagation, not back-propagation). If the cost function or the accuracy of your model is much worse on the test set, then either

  1. You have not performed a good split between training data and test data—this is usually achieved by shuffling the items in the dataset before the split to guarantee a more uniform distribution of the data.

  2. The network hasn't been presented with enough data points to efficiently detect patterns in your dataset—you can fix it by adding more data points.

  3. The dataset contains too many features: you may want to apply principal component analysis or any type of dimensionality reduction algorithm to remove the features that are either redundant (linear combinations of other features) or don't really influence the distribution and patterns of your data.

  4. The network overfits the points in the training set. In this case, you may want to either experiment with a network with a lower number of units/layers or pick a higher value for the regularization rate λ in order to increase the "inertia" of the network against the "swings" in your dataset.

As we have seen, once we have found a way toward convergence given a training set, we have mainly two parameters that we can tune to adjust the performance of the model: the learning rate α and the regularization rate λ. We have seen that α determines how fast the network learns when presented with new data and λ expresses the "resistance" of the network against change. Sometimes the dataset is split into three instead of two in order to separately adjust these two values:

- First, we train the model on the *training set* and make sure that its cost function constantly decreases. The goal of this phase is to find the values of the weights Θ that minimize the cost function and a value of α (or a function $\alpha(t)$ that returns α over the iteration t) that is a reasonable trade-off between speed and robustness (expressed as the tendency of the model to converge regardless of the starting point).

- Then, we use the *cross-validation set* to adjust λ. The goal of this phase is to pick a value of λ (or a function $\lambda(t)$ that returns λ over the iteration t) that is a reasonable trade-off between underfit and overfit.

- Finally, we evaluate the model on the *test set* to evaluate the overall performance of the model on data points that it hasn't seen yet. We evaluate both the cost function and any accessory performance metrics of the model on this data and use them to establish whether the model performs well enough or it requires more training, a different parameter tuning, or a different architecture.

Another good practice is to write small tests to check the performance of your model. So far we have covered the mathematical tools that help us perform quantitative analysis on the overall performance of the model, but in a real-world problem, you may have a clearer idea of what your model should predict in specific cases. So pick a few cases both significant enough and diverse enough from your data and write some tests that measure how many of those cases the model got right or wrong. This is a useful tool to effectively keep track of the evolution of your model over time. Use such tests to see if a specific change in your model leads to a better classification for these "core cases" and to make sure that later changes to the model don't deteriorate its performance on these data points.

Another general good practice is to keep in mind that machine learning models are still pieces of software, and like any other piece of software, they should go through a similar process. Using tools like Jupyter notebooks to interactively visualize the data and train your models adds a lot of value and productivity to the process, but keep in mind that the output of your work shouldn't be only a model file, trained by a notebook that will be either tossed away or saved on a personal laptop. The output of your work when you train a model should include, besides the model file:

- A clean (and preferably versioned) codebase that can be reused to re-train the model, debug it, or train different models. Extract the common parts of your codebase (like saving and loading models, normalizing the data, or initializing a classifier) into reusable modules that can be easily imported so you won't have to reinvent the wheel or go down the path of scarcely maintainable copy/paste. Make scripts out of your notebooks, so the training, evaluation, and prediction phases can be easily run on other systems as stand-alone entities, without requiring the Jupyter environment.

- Tests for your model, following the guidelines previously described.

- Keep in mind that in a real-case application your model is usually a block in the chain of a larger business logic. In a real application, you usually generate or ingest data from somewhere, run some custom logic on this data, use your machine learning model to make some prediction on the data, and use those predictions to run some additional business logic. So it's good to keep in mind that, just like any other module in a more complex system, it's good to design your machine learning logic with scalability and inter-communication in mind. Reading from a CSV file and printing the results on the standard output is a good way to debug and test your model, but in a real application, you may want to wrap your model into, for instance, a WSGI or Flask web application so it's easy to use it over, for example, a REST API. Or design it in a way that it can consume queries or training/evaluation commands from a message queue or a WebSocket. You may even consider deploying it as a Docker microservice if it needs to be deployed on multiple environments so you don't have to directly install all the dependencies on the target system—and usually it also helps preventing the "but it works on my laptop" issue.

- Whenever possible, keep track of the data used to train your model. The increased number of applications of machine learning in the past few years has been accompanied by an increasing number of issues related to bad predictions resulting from bad/biased data. Companies that train their models on huge amounts of data struggle to keep track of which biased training inputs led to which biased classifications, and machine learning models are often treated as black-box oracles—we know what they predict, but we can't tell why exactly they made those predictions. That's why it's increasingly important to keep track of the data that you use to train your models and preferably version it/tag it: it makes it easier to pinpoint at the root cause in case of degradation of the model's performance, and it also helps increasing the accountability of the model.

2.3 Error metrics

We have so far analyzed a few metrics to evaluate the performance of a model. Among those are the following:

- *Mean squared error*, often used as the driving cost function of the model in regression problems

- *Mean absolute error*, sometimes used as an additional performance metric

- *Classification error*, used as a driving cost function both in logistic regression and neural networks

- *Accuracy*, defined as number of correct classifications divided by the total number of samples, and probably one of the most popular performance metrics

Accuracy, however, doesn't always give an accurate picture of how well the model performs for a specific problem. Suppose that you want to train a model that detects whether a user who registers to your website is a potential bot/scammer/fraudster. In a normal scenario, such users may represent just a minority of the traffic on your website, and therefore, your dataset may picture a situation where 99% of the users are regular users and 1% of them are fake. In such a scenario, you may gain *accuracy* = 99% with this simple function:

```
def is_fake(user):
    return False
```

The problem with accuracy is that it fails to provide a good picture of the actual performance of a model when the classification problem involves *skewed* classes—that is, classes with very different distributions, often associated to anomaly detection problems or generally to problems that involve the prediction of rare events.

For such cases, it usually helps a more granular approach than looking at the overall accuracy. For simplicity, let's consider a binary classification problem: $y = 0$ identifies a negative data point and $y = 1$ a positive one. Our model makes a prediction for each data point—either $h_\Theta(\bar{x}) = 0$ (negative prediction) or $h_\Theta(\bar{x}) = 1$ (positive prediction). We can define the following metrics on the basis of the predicted values:

1. *True positives* (**TP**): Data points labelled as positive and predicted as positive ($y = 1$ and $h_\Theta(\bar{x}) = 1$)

2. *True negatives* (**TN**): Data points labelled as negative and predicted as negative ($y = 1$ and $h_\Theta(\bar{x}) = 1$)

3. *False positives* (**FP**): Data points labelled as negative but predicted as positive ($y = 0$ and $h_\Theta(\bar{x}) = 1$)

4. *False negatives* (**FN**): Data points labelled as positive but predicted as negative ($y = 1$ and $h_\Theta(\bar{x}) = 0$)

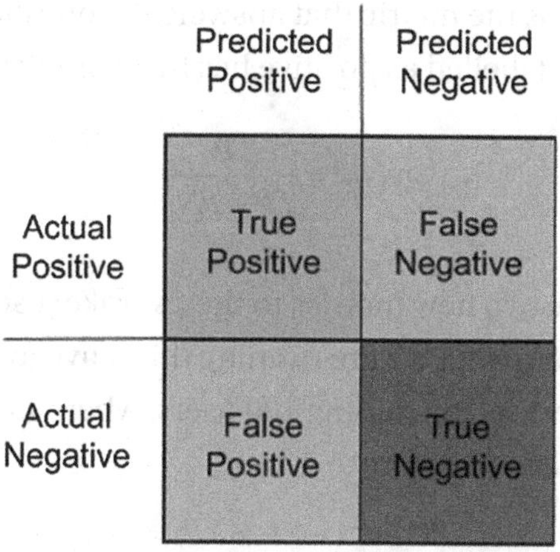

Figure 2-6. *Structure of a confusion matrix. Each cell reports the number of items that fit that selected category after a run of validation of the model*

Usually these metrics are visualized in a *confusion matrix* with a structure like the one shown in Figure 2-6.

With this new formalism, we can define the accuracy of the model as follows:

$$accuracy = \frac{TP + TN}{TP + TN + FP + FN}$$

Accuracy is the metric that answers the question "Which fraction of the available items has been correctly classified?"

We define **precision** as the metric that answers the question "Which fraction of the items predicted as positive is actually positive?"

$$precision = \frac{TP}{TP + FP}$$

While the **recall** is the metric that answers the question "Which fraction of the items labelled as positive has been predicted as positive?"

$$recall = \frac{TP}{TP + FN}$$

Let's apply these two new metrics to the is_fake(user) function shown before. Suppose that we are running this naive model that always returns *False* on a test set containing 100 users, where 1 of them is *fake* and 99 are regular. We have therefore

- $TP = 0$

- $TN = 99$

- $FP = 0$

- $FN = 1$

And

- $accuracy = \frac{0+99}{0+99+0+1} = 99\%$

- $precision = \frac{0}{0+0} = N / A$

- $recall = \frac{0}{0+1} = 0\%$

A recall value of 0 clearly says that something is wrong with the classifier, even though the overall accuracy is 99%. Note that precision and recall aren't always measurable: in some limit cases, like our naive is_fake(user) function, the denominator may be zero—but at least one of the two metrics is usually computable.

You can use these two additional metrics to better evaluate the performance of your model and optimize performance in classification problems with skewed classes—even at the cost of a trade-off on overall accuracy if required. You can also find trade-offs between these two metrics based on your business logic. Suppose that your model predicts whether a patient has a cancer on the basis of X-ray images: you can optimize either its precision or its recall based on the answer you give to the question *is it worse to tell healthy patients that they have cancer, or tell patients with cancer that they are healthy?*

If your model detects potential intrusions from the camera images in a bank, you may want to optimize recall—if the cost of a real intrusion is very high, then it might be safe to ensure that any potential intrusion is detected, even at the cost of a higher number of false positives. If instead your model sends notifications to all the employees in a department about potential spikes of traffic on a certain system, you may want to prefer precision over recall—send a notification when we're pretty confident that there is a spike to prevent spamming the employees with false positives.

Sometimes a metric that combines both precision and recall is used to evaluate the performance of a model: the **F1 score** is defined as the *harmonic mean* of precision and recall and is often used as a more granular accuracy metric:

$$F_1 = 2\frac{PR}{P+R}$$

To summarize, so far we have covered

- The intuition behind neural networks, how to use them to make predictions (forward-propagation), and how to train them (back-propagation)

- How to evaluate the quality of the training process—measures to prevent underfit and overfit, normalization, regularization, and feature selection

- Which are the best practices to debug, test, design, package, and distribute our machine learning models

- Which accessory performance metrics can be used to evaluate the model if we have skewed classes or we want to detect anomalies

We now have all the ingredients to start getting our hands dirty with some code.

2.4 Implementing a network to recognize clothing items

Nowadays it's relatively easy to implement neural networks using libraries like TensorFlow and Keras. I won't cover a full implementation from scratch in Python of forward-propagation and back-propagation like I did for regression, but even if you're unlikely to find yourself in a situation where you have to implement the full-blown algorithm yourself, I strongly encourage you to try and implement it from scratch, to make sure that you grasp all the intuitions behind. After all, it wasn't that long ago that developers had to implement these algorithms themselves—I believe that my 12-year-old library for neural networks in C++ is still lost somewhere on the old Google Code portal. Even if initializing, compiling, and training a model can be done in three lines of Python code nowadays, the framework doesn't take care of normalizing the data, and the methods provided by TensorFlow and Keras still require some tuning and knowledge about how the algorithms work, if you want to get your model to work in a real-world application.

In this section, we'll cover an example often considered as the new hello world of neural networks: the Fashion MNIST dataset originally uploaded by Zalando. The traditional MNIST dataset has been used for many years to introduce students to machine learning, and it includes

116

a large list of images with handwritten and labelled digits. The Fashion MNIST dataset adds a bit more complexity on top of the original problem—you'll have to train a model that detects clothing items from pictures. The Fashion MNIST dataset is provided by default on a typical TensorFlow+Keras installation, and you can load it like this into your notebook:

```
import tensorflow as tf
from tensorflow import keras

fashion_mnist = keras.datasets.fashion_mnist
(train_images, train_labels), (test_images, test_labels) = \
    fashion_mnist.load_data()
```

There are ten types of clothing included in the dataset, but their classes aren't directly provided as strings. You can initialize an array with the associated class names:

```
class_names = ['T-shirt/top', 'Trouser', 'Pullover', 'Dress',
               'Coat', 'Sandal', 'Shirt', 'Sneaker', 'Bag',
               'Ankle boot']
```

By taking a look at the data, we notice that the training set contains 60,000 images, while the test set contains 10,000 images—in both cases, we are dealing with 28x28 pixel black and white images:

```
train_images.shape
# Output: (60000, 28, 28)
test_images.shape
# Output: (10000, 28, 28)
```

And when it comes to the labels, their values are in range 0–9 and can be mapped to our class_names vector:

```
train_labels
# Output: array([9, 0, 0, ..., 3, 0, 5], dtype=uint8)
test_labels
# Output: array([9, 2, 1, ..., 8, 1, 5], dtype=uint8)
```

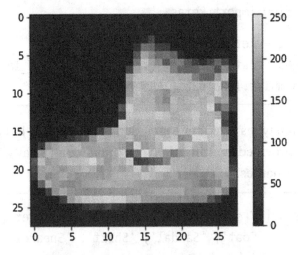

Figure 2-7. *Histogram of an image from the Fashion MNIST dataset*

When we deal with images, the first thing we want to do is take a look at some of the images in the dataset to get hints about the color space, range, and look: the images in this dataset are already trimmed to include only the clothing item, but in a real-world scenario, you're likely to be provided with large datasets that require some form of preprocessing (like trimming, downscaling, or color transformation) before being fed to a neural network:

```
import matplotlib.pyplot as plt

plt.figure()
plt.imshow(train_images[0])
plt.colorbar()
plt.grid(False)
plt.show()
```

You'll see a picture like the one shown in Figure 2-7. We are dealing with black and white images, the information about each pixel is encoded in one byte, and therefore each pixel has a value between 0 (black) and 255 (white). The first step when it comes to models that operate on images is to normalize them—and in the case of black and white images, this is usually done by applying a transformation that translates the [0,255] range into a [0.0,1.0] range:

```
def normalize(images):
    return images / 255.0

train_images = normalize(train_images)
test_images = normalize(test_images)
```

A quick note about the color space. When it comes to models dealing with images, it's quite important to pick the right color space if you really want to boost performance. While RGB is the most common option to export images, it's not necessarily the best format to train a model. Before settling on a specific color space for your model, ask yourself this question: what kind of information or pattern do I want to detect in these images? If your neural network is supposed to be used in a self-driving car to recognize the colors of traffic lights, then RGB is a good pick. If you want to detect shapes against a background, black and white is usually a better pick—it not only makes the model simpler and faster but also more robust, as different pictures of the same object or shape may show different colors depending on lighting or environment conditions. Other application may perform better with more exotic color spaces. If your model is supposed to recognize lighting conditions in a room, for instance, then color spaces that take luminosity into account (like YUV or YCbCr) can perform better than RGB or grayscale. In other applications where the patterns depend on how much color or saturation the images have, color spaces that take those metrics into account (like HSL and HSV) can be the best pick. Always keep in mind that the color space that you choose influences the pattern that the network is able to infer. Not only that, but also choose the right source of data for your model depending on what your model is supposed to recognize. Images from an optical camera work well if you want to classify objects. If instead you want to detect the presence of people, then an infrared or thermal camera could provide better performance, because the images from an optical camera would have a lot of variability—a person can be standing, sitting, or lying in different positions in different parts of a room, and you could also have multiple people in the same room, while an infrared camera would only provide you with the information your model actually needs: "Are there any human-shaped sources of heat around 36–37°C in the image?" In other applications, you may want to rely on more inputs: a model that detects the presence of people can be way more accurate if you also integrate data from microphones or other environment sensors.

Machine learning is often described as a process where you feed data to a model and the model "learns" by itself, but the reality is more complex than that. Choosing the right source of information, collecting data, removing the redundant information, trimming and transforming the data, detecting any potential source of bias, and normalizing the data actually make 90% of the performance of your model. The mathematics we have explored so far is often implemented in libraries and frameworks nowadays; it is relatively complex, but you won't have to implement it from scratch (even if that doesn't mean that you don't need to understand how these models work under the hood). What really matters nowadays is the quality of the data you use and how good you have been at collecting it even before you write the first line of code. Machine learning isn't like feeding data to a model and let the model learn by itself. It's more similar to the way penguins feed their offspring—the adult penguin is in charge of fishing, chewing, and pre-digesting the food before feeding it to their young ones.

That being said, let's proceed with our classifier of clothes. A good idea is to take a look at how a bunch of images look in the dataset and what's their classification:

```
plt.figure(figsize=(10,10))

# Plot the first 25 images and their
# associated classes in a 5x5 grid
for i in range(25):
    plt.subplot(5,5,i+1)
    plt.xticks([])
    plt.yticks([])
    plt.grid(False)
    plt.imshow(train_images[i], cmap=plt.cm.binary)
    plt.xlabel(class_names[train_labels[i]])

plt.show()
```

Figure 2-8. *Sampling the first 25 images of the Fashion MNIST dataset*

You should see a figure like the one shown in Figure 2-8.

If the classification looks right and the data is normalized, let's proceed with building a neural network classifier. This is usually done in Keras using the Sequential model that links together multiple custom layers. Usually a model that works on image classification problems has the following structure:

1. An input layer that contains as many units as the number of pixels of each image. We have seen, however, that the input layer of a network is a one-dimensional vector of units, while here we are dealing with two-dimensional images. The first layer therefore is usually of type Flatten, and it "unfolds" the two-dimensional images into one-dimensional arrays that can be propagated into the next layers. We have seen that the images in the Fashion MNIST dataset are 28x28 pixel images: it means that our first layer will have $28 \times 28 = 784$ units.

2. An output layer that has as many units as the number of classes that we want to detect. In our cases, 10 classes means 10 units in the output layer, and the unit with the highest activation value is the one we want to associate to a specific data point.

3. A variable number of hidden layers between the input and output layer with a variable number of units. We have previously seen that increasing the number of intermediate units and layers is a good way of improving the accuracy of your model, but increasing it too much may lead to overfit—and you can usually overcome it either by tuning the number of units and layers until you reach a satisfying trade-off between the accuracy on the training set and test set or by increasing the regularization rate so the network is more tightly "anchored." We will use both for the output layer and for the intermediate layers the Dense Keras layer type, which initializes a layer such that each of its units is connected to each of the units both in the previous and next layer.

Putting all together, let's proceed with writing the code that initializes our model:

```
model = keras.Sequential([
    keras.layers.Flatten(input_shape=(28, 28)),
    keras.layers.Dense(500, activation='sigmoid'),
    keras.layers.Dense(200, activation='sigmoid'),
    keras.layers.Dense(10, activation='softmax')
    ])
```

This code defines a network with one input layer, two hidden layers, and one output layer (`keras.Sequential`). The first layer takes our normalized 28 × 28 image vectors as inputs and transforms them into one-dimensional vectors (`keras.Flatten`). The two hidden layers, respectively, contain 500 and 200 units (feel free to experiment with the number of units and hidden layers and see how it affects the model). They use a `sigmoid` activation function—the same one we have explored so far. The output layer has 10 units—as many as the number of classes. The value of each unit will express the probability for a given input image to belong to that class. We may want to use the `softmax` activation function for the output layer whenever we have multiple classes, and we want to express the value of each unit as a probability/confidence level.

Next, just like in the regression models, we want to *compile* this model so it's ready to be trained:

```
model.compile(optimizer='adam',
    loss=tf.keras.losses.SparseCategoricalCrossentropy(
    from_logits=True),
    # or loss='categorical_crossentropy',
    metrics=['accuracy'])
```

Digging on what's happening here:

- We use adam as an optimizer for the network, a first-order gradient-based optimization algorithm first proposed in 2014 that has gained quite some popularity over the past years for training deep neural networks. We have covered already other optimizers in the chapter on regression. Many of them—stochastic gradient descent (SGD), nadam, RMSprop, and so on—are also commonly used for neural networks. Again, the best way to get a grasp of the optimizers is to read about those most commonly used and experiment which one performs better on your data.

- We then define a cost function that we want to minimize using the optimizer (like we have seen already in the case of regression, the Keras framework names them as *loss functions* instead of cost functions, but they basically mean the same thing). While mean squared error (or mean logarithmic squared error) is a common choice for linear regression problems, cross-entropy functions are a common choice for classification problems—including logistic regression and classification through neural networks. The concept of cross-entropy is very close to the types of cost functions $J\left(\overline{\theta}\right)$ we have analyzed in our classification problems. In general, in information theory, the cross-entropy between two distributions p and q over the same set of events represents the average number of bits (or pieces of information) required to "convert" p into q. If p and q are, respectively, our expected and predicted values for a certain set of data

125

points, then the cross-entropy intuitively measures how "distant" our set of predictions is from the set of expected values—or how many bits in average we need to change so that our predictions match the expectations. Another way to look at cross-entropy is in probabilistic terms: you can see it as a measure of how likely your predictions are to be right. You would usually use a binary cross-entropy loss function if you are building a model for true/false predictions. In our case, we want to make prediction over multiple classes, so a categorical or sparse categorical cross-entropy function would usually be a popular choice.

- Like in the case of regression, we want to define one or more additional metrics as "health" metrics to make sure that the model is actually learning and not overfitting the data points according to the provided cost function. In this case, like we did in the case of regression, we use accuracy, but keep in mind that depending on the distribution of your data (especially in the case of skewed datasets) and the trade-off you want to achieve between false positive and false negatives, you can also use precision and recall or any other metric.

Then, like we have seen in the case of regression, we use the fit method to train our compiled model over the training set:

```
history = model.fit(train_images, train_labels, epochs=10)
```

In this case, we specified 10 iterations over the data points. Again, remember that the number of epochs can determine whether your model will underfit, overfit, or "just" fit the data, so you may want to look at the output of your notebook to see how the performance of the model changes over the epochs:

```
Epoch 1/10
1875/1875 [======] - 6s 3ms/step - loss: 0.5423 - accuracy: 0.8091
Epoch 2/10
1875/1875 [======] - 6s 3ms/step - loss: 0.3781 - accuracy: 0.8621
Epoch 3/10
1875/1875 [======] - 7s 4ms/step - loss: 0.3396 - accuracy: 0.8755
Epoch 4/10
1875/1875 [======] - 7s 4ms/step - loss: 0.3144 - accuracy: 0.8842
Epoch 5/10
1875/1875 [======] - 9s 5ms/step - loss: 0.2956 - accuracy: 0.8912
Epoch 6/10
1875/1875 [======] - 7s 4ms/step - loss: 0.2805 - accuracy: 0.8961
Epoch 7/10
1875/1875 [======] - 7s 4ms/step - loss: 0.2649 - accuracy: 0.9014
Epoch 8/10
1875/1875 [======] - 7s 4ms/step - loss: 0.2508 - accuracy: 0.9062
Epoch 9/10
1875/1875 [======] - 7s 4ms/step - loss: 0.2387 - accuracy: 0.9105
Epoch 10/10
1875/1875 [======] - 8s 4ms/step - loss: 0.2303 - accuracy: 0.9128
```

A few common rules of thumb to interpret your metrics:

- It's important that your loss/cost function consistently goes down over the epochs. If it doesn't visibly race toward zero, then you may want to normalize/improve your training data. If it goes up and down, then the cost function may have some "bumps"—either review your data or tune the learning rate, the regularization rate, or the optimizer. If you don't notice great improvements after some point, it means that the cost function already converged earlier and you can reduce the number of epochs, or you could run into overfit issues.

- While the cost function is expected to consistently decrease, your secondary metrics (accuracy, precision, or recall) are expected to consistently increase. If they don't, then you may want to investigate possible overfit issues or tune learning/regularization rate.

You can also plot how the accuracy of your model changes over the training epochs:

```
epochs = history.epoch
accuracy = history.history['accuracy']

fig = plt.figure()
plot = fig.add_subplot()
plot.set_xlabel('epoch')
plot.set_ylabel('accuracy')
plot.plot(epochs, accuracy)
```

Once we are happy with the performance metrics of the training phase, it's time to evaluate the newly trained model over the test set:

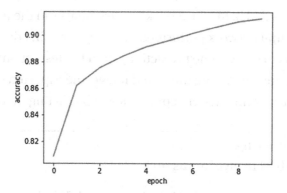

Figure 2-9. *Progress of the model accuracy over 10 training epochs*

```
test_loss, test_acc = model.evaluate(test_images, test_
labels, verbose=2)
```

You will probably see an output like this:

```
313/313 - 1s - loss: 0.3185 - accuracy: 0.8871
```

And plotting the accuracy over the epochs should result in a graph like the one shown in Figure 2-9.

What this means is that our model has an 88.71% probability of guessing the class correctly on a test set of 313 items. That is about 2.5% less than the accuracy achieved on the last training iteration if we compare it with the previous output. In a real-case scenario, it's up to you (or those in charge of the project) to make the call whether such results are good enough. If the accuracy over the test set diverges too much from the accuracy over the training set, then, again, you may want to investigate overfit. It's also a good practice to increase the number of samples in the test set in order to make more statistically significant observations.

It's now a good idea to take a peek at a few images in the test set and see how the neural network performed on them. Let's first define a few utility functions to show some predictions from the test set onto a grid, with each element containing the tested image, the expected label, the predicted label, and the model's confidence in predicting that label:

```python
import numpy as np
import matplotlib.pyplot as plt

# Plot the image, the predicted/expected label
# and the confidence level
def plot_image_and_predictions(prediction, classes, true_
label, img):
    plt.grid(False)
    plt.xticks([])
    plt.yticks([])
    plt.imshow(img, cmap=plt.cm.binary)
    predicted_label = int(np.argmax(prediction))
    confidence = 100 * np.max(prediction)
    color = 'blue' if predicted_label == true_label else 'red'

plt.xlabel('{predicted} {confidence:2.0f}% ({expected})'.format(
    predicted=classes[predicted_label],
    confidence=confidence,
    expected=classes[int(true_label)]), color=color)

# Plot a bar chart with the confidence level of each label
def plot_value_array(prediction, true_label):
    plt.grid(False)
    plt.xticks([])
    plt.yticks([])
    thisplot = plt.bar(range(len(prediction)), prediction,
    color="#777777")
```

```
plt.ylim([0, 1])
predicted_label = np.argmax(prediction)

thisplot[predicted_label].set_color('red')
thisplot[true_label].set_color('blue')

# Plot the first N test images, their predicted and expected
label.
# It colors correct predictions in blue, incorrect predictions
in red.
def plot_results(images, labels, predictions, classes, rows,
cols):
    n_images = rows * cols
    plt.figure(figsize=(2 * 2 * cols, 2 * rows))

    for i in range(n_images):
        plt.subplot(rows, 2 * cols, 2 * i + 1)
        plot_image_and_predictions(predictions[i], classes,
                                    labels[i], images[i])
        plt.subplot(rows, 2 * cols, 2 * i + 2)
        plot_value_array(predictions[i], labels[i])

    plt.show()

# predictions will contain the predicted values for the test set
predictions = model.predict(test_images)

# Plot the predictions for the first 25 values of the test set
plot_results(images=test_images, labels=test_labels,
classes=class_names,
            predictions=predictions, rows=5, cols=5)
```

You will probably see a figure like the one shown in Figure 2-10. This kind of visualization applied to the test set helps you understand how the network performs on images that are not in the training set, and you can use it to spot common patterns that can help you improve your model—like categories of items that are commonly mislabelled or with a "close call" error margin. You may want to use this kind of visualization to refine your input data, improve your images preprocessing pipeline, or tweak the model with the strategies seen so far (tuning learning rate, normalization rate, number of neurons, number of epochs, cost function, etc.) to improve the performance until you are satisfied.

Figure 2-10. *Plotting the predicted classes for the first 25 images in the test set, together with the expected labels and the classification confidence levels*

Once you are satisfied with your model, don't forget to save it. The procedure is the same we have seen previously for saving TensorFlow regression models:

```
def model_save(model_dir, labels, overwrite=True):
    import json
    import os

    # Create the model directory if it doesn't exist
    os.makedirs(model_dir, exist_ok=True)
```

```
    # The TensorFlow model save won't keep track of the
    # labels of your model.  It's usually a good practice to
    # store them in a separate JSON file.
    labels_file = os.path.join(model_dir, 'labels.json')
    with open(labels_file, 'w') as f:
        f.write(json.dumps(list(labels)))

    # Then, save the TensorFlow model using the save primitive
    model.save(model_dir, overwrite=overwrite)

model_dir = '/home/user/models/fashion-mnist'
model_save(model_dir, labels=class_names)
```

Similarly, you can load the saved model from your application without going through the training phase again:

```
def model_load(model_dir):
    import json
    import os
    from tensorflow.keras.models import load_model

    labels = []
    labels_file = os.path.join(model_dir, 'labels.json')

    if os.path.isfile(labels_file):
        with open(labels_file) as f:
            labels = json.load(f)

    m = load_model(model_dir)
    return m, labels

model, labels = model_load(model_dir)
```

Congratulations on training and saving your first neural network for image classification!

2.5 Convolutional neural networks

The Fashion MNIST dataset is perfect for introducing neural networks, but it's simpler than many real-world datasets of images. The network was trained on a set of preprocessed 28x28 monochrome images all containing exactly the item supposed to be identified—in many real-world scenarios, you won't usually deal with such neatly trimmed datasets. Ideally, we want to build models robust enough to classify items also when we input some image with feature slightly different than the one the model was trained on—in particular, we want our model to be robust against trimming, rotations, and small amounts of blurring or color/luminosity changes.

Convolutional neural networks (or **CNNs**) come a step closer to the way the human brain processes images. When they perform a visual classification or interpretation of the environment around, our brains don't simply feed the raw luminosity and color signals delivered over the optical nerve uniformly to all the areas in the visual cortex. Such an organization would require lots of biological energy, since all the input neurons of the cortex would be active all the time, and a huge number of downstream connections would be required as well. Instead, the input signals are initially preprocessed by an area of the visual cortex known as *receptive field* [16] [17]. A receptive field acts like a filter that preprocesses some input signals. It discards the information that isn't required; it adjusts/ normalizes the data against, for example, environment luminosity and orientation; and finally it identifies some *features* or patterns (determined by, e.g., edges, luminosity areas, or spatial features) that should fire some particular neurons downstream. The sensory networks of most mammals are designed to detect patterns and detect them fast, focusing on the most relevant elements in the surrounding environments while discarding information that isn't required, and they are modelled to be robust enough in their job also in varying situations of luminosity, distance, and orientation. Studies on primates have proved that certain receptive fields are in charge of filtering and normalizing sensory signals in varying situations of luminosity and orientation, and that when presented to the same object under varying conditions of luminosity, the signals delivered by those receptive fields to the downstream neurons were similar—in other words, the receptive field in the visual cortex of the animal was in charge of *normalizing* the data and making sure that the process of visual classification was independent on the luminosity of the environment [18].

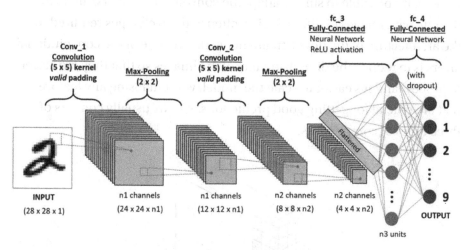

Figure 2-11. *Typical architecture of a convolutional neural network. The image shows its convolutional layers (used for feature extraction), pooling layers (used for dimensionality reduction), flattening layer, and the downstream fully connected neural network (used for classification) (Credits: Towards Data Science [19])*

CNNs can be seen as an artificial application of this principle. In a CNN, a set of filters is applied to the original image in order to extract features such as shapes and color areas and reduce the initial complexity. Those features are then fed to a traditional neural network. Since the neural network operates on sets of extracted features instead of raw sets of pixels, these networks usually perform better at classifying images than an equivalent neural network of the same size but without convolutional layers, as they are better at capturing spatial and temporal dependencies

135

between the areas in an image. Also, CNNs scale much better when the size of the input samples increases. The network we designed in the previous example had exactly as many input units as the number of pixels in the image. Making the network work with larger images involves either scaling down the images or increasing the number of units in the input layer—that, in turn, usually involves re-training the model. In a CNN instead, it's possible to simply adapt the convolutional layers/filters to operate with images of different size, often with no changes required to the architecture of the downstream network. The role of the convolutional layers is to reduce the dimensionality of the images so that they are easier to process and it's easier to scale the model, without losing any features that are crucial for getting good predictions. A CNN usually consists of three types of components:

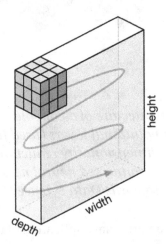

Figure 2-12. *Movement of a kernel/filter tensor in a convolutional layer over the original image (Credits: Towards Data Science [19])*

1. One or more **convolutional layers**, whose job is
    to iteratively apply a transformation to the input
    image through a matrix/tensor known as **filter** or
    kernel. The purpose of a convolutional layer is to
    capture higher-level features in the input image by
    looking not only at the information stored in each
    pixel but also at the relationships between each
    pixel and its "neighborhood" (e.g., Is it on an edge?
    Do surrounding pixels have different levels of color/
    luminosity?). The sophistication of the extracted
    features increases as we add more and more
    convolutional layers. The first layer would usually
    capture low-level features such as edges, color
    gradients, and orientation, while the downstream
    layers will spot more complex features such as
    objects, sizes, distances, and so on.

2. One or more **pooling layers**, whose input
    units are usually linked to the output units of a
    convolutional layers. Their job is to further reduce
    the dimensionality of the input data and select
    the dominant features extracted by the upstream
    convolutional layers, especially those that are
    invariant to transformations such as rotations or
    translations—the purpose of a pooling layer is
    functionally similar to the principal component
    analysis algorithm we have analyzed earlier.

3. Finally, the matrix/tensor of features extracted from
    the original data is flattened and fed into a fully
    connected neural network that will perform the
    classification process.

The final high-level architecture of such a network is shown in Figure 2-11. Let's analyze its layers one by one.

2.5.1 Convolutional layer

An input image is usually provided as a $w \times h \times c$ matrix/tensor, where w and h are, respectively, its width and height and c is the depth of its color space (1 in the case of monochrome images, 3 in the case of RGB/HSV/YUV, etc.). A *filter* or *kernel* matrix/tensor K sized $m \times n \times c$, with $m < h$ and $n < h$, is either statically encoded in the layer or dynamically calculated. K is shifted over the whole image, as shown in Figure 2-12. On each iteration, the kernel moves from left to right if there are more pixels to be processed in a row and from top to bottom otherwise (changing the direction to right to left on the next row), until the whole image is processed. On each iteration, the top-left element of K, k_{00}, will be aligned with the (i,j) pixel of the input matrix A, a_{ij}, with $0 \le i < h$ and $0 \le j < w$. Let us define A_{ij} as the subset of A covered by K:

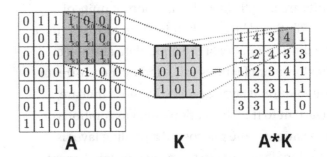

Figure 2-13. *An example of 2D convolution operation between a monochrome input image A and a kernel K*

$$A_{ij} = \begin{bmatrix} a_{ij} & a_{(i+1)j} & \cdots & a_{(i+m-1)j} \\ a_{i(j+1)} & a_{(i+1)(j+1)} & \cdots & a_{(i+m-1)(j+1)} \\ \vdots & \vdots & \ddots & \vdots \\ a_{i(j+n-1)} & a_{(i+1)(j+n-1)} & \cdots & a_{(i+m-1)(j+n-1)} \end{bmatrix}$$

Both A_{ij} and K are tensors sized $m \times n \times c$—even if the preceding formula shows for simplicity each pixel as a single number and therefore A_{ij} is shown as a 2D matrix. We can then define the convolution operation between the subset of the image covered by the kernel and the kernel itself, $A_{ij} * K$, as the sum of the element-wise products between the elements of A_{ij} and K:

$$A_{ij} * K = \sum_{x=0}^{m-1} \sum_{y=0}^{n-1} \sum_{z=0}^{c-1} a_{xyz} * k_{xyz}$$

This operation resembles quite closely the element-wise vector product (or *Hadamard product*) we have seen in the back-propagation algorithm, and a 2D example is shown in Figure 2-13. In Python, you could write it as follows:

```python
def conv_product(A, K):
    conv = 0.0
    for x in range(len(K)):
        for y in range(len(K[0])):
            for z in range(len(K[0][0])):
                conv += A[x][y][z] * K[x][y][z]

    return conv
```

The convolutional tensor *Conv* between the whole image *A* and the kernel *K* can be calculated by applying the "snake-like" motion shown in Figure 2-12:

$$conv_{ij} = A_{ij} * K \text{ for } 0 \le i < w - m, 0 \le j < h - n$$

In Python:

```python
def submatrix(A, i, j, m, n):
    # Calculate the submatrix of a matrix A starting from the
    # element (i, j) up to (i+m, j+n)
    return [
        [
            A[i][j]
            for j in range(j, j+n)
        ]
        for i in range(i, i+m)
    ]

def conv(A, K):
    # The result will be a (w-m)*(h-n) matrix
    return [
        [
            conv_product(submatrix(A, i, j, len(K), len(K[0])), K)
            for j in range(len(A[0])-len(K[0])+1)
        ]
        for i in range(len(A)-len(K)+1)
    ]
```

Such kernels and filters have been used for a long time in computer vision. One of the most popular ones is arguably the *Sobel map,* or *Sobel-Feldman operator* [20]. This filter is actually composed of two

3×3 matrices, S_x and S_y, used to calculate an approximation for the luminosity/color gradient, respectively, for the x and y dimension:

$$S_x = \begin{bmatrix} 1 & 0 & -1 \\ 2 & 0 & -2 \\ 1 & 0 & -1 \end{bmatrix}$$

$$S_y = S_x^T = \begin{bmatrix} 1 & 2 & 1 \\ 0 & 0 & 0 \\ 1 & -2 & -1 \end{bmatrix}$$

The results of the convolution operations between these matrices and the original image, respectively, approximate the x and y color gradient of the image around a particular point:

$$G_x = A * S_x$$
$$G_y = A * S_y$$

Figure 2-14. *Example of the Sobel kernel applied to an image. Each pixel in the right image represents the magnitude of the convolution operation between the Sobel maps and the associated pixel in the original image. Pixels on the edge of objects are brighter than the others*

The modulus of this vector represents the magnitude of the gradient vector in a particular point in the image—the higher the value, the more likely the point is to belong to the edge of an object in an image:

$$G = \sqrt{G_x^2 + G_y^2}$$

The phase of the vector instead identifies the direction of the gradient in a particular point—and that can be used to tell on which side of an edge pixel an object lies:

$$\Theta = \operatorname{atan}\left(\frac{G_y}{G_x}\right)$$

The kernels used in the convolutional layer are akin to the Sobel maps (some may even use the Sobel maps for edge detection), and just like a Sobel map, they can be used to detect features such as edges and gradients in images (see example in Figure 2-14).

Finally, besides the choice of the kernel and its size, two more coefficients that can be tuned in a convolutional layer are as follows:

1. *Stride*: It determines how much the kernel should shift over the image on each iteration of the convolutional product. In the examples we have seen in this paragraph, the kernel had a stride of 1—we moved it over the image one position at the time—and this is also the most commonly used value. Larger strides will result in smaller output tensors. A larger stride can be used to perform greater dimensional reduction, as long as you keep in mind that very large values have higher chances of discarding useful information.

2. *Padding*: The original image can either be processed
   directly through the convolutional operation or
   padded with zeros before the operation. In this
   paragraph, we have shown examples of **valid
   padding** (or no padding)—the original matrices/
   tensors were not padded before applying the
   convolution. If instead you add two rows of zeros to
   the top and bottom and two columns of zeros to the
   left and right of the images, you will be performing
   what is called **same padding**. Valid padding
   performs dimensional reduction as well as feature
   extraction (the output tensor will be smaller than
   the input), while same padding performs feature
   extraction but keeps the same dimensions.

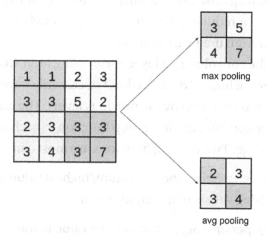

Figure 2-15. *Example results of a 2 × 2 max and average pooling
operation applied to an input 2D matrix*

You can therefore tune *stride* and *padding* to tune how much the layer should reduce the dimensions of the input image before passing the output tensor to the next layers. A configuration with stride = 1 and same padding results in no actual reduction of the dimensions, and in that case, you may want to perform the reduction entirely on the pooling layer downstream.

2.5.2 Pooling layer

The output of a convolutional layer is usually connected to a *pooling layer*. The purpose of the pooling layer is to reduce the dimensionality of the tensor while possibly not losing any relevant information needed for a correct classification. Moreover, it is useful to extract the features of an image that are invariant with regard to rotation and position, making the model more robust against image transformations. Finally, it acts as a *noise reducer*, removing or reducing the impact on the model of noisy pixels that are too dissimilar from their surroundings.

Similarly to the convolutional layer, the pooling layer works by shifting a $m \times n$ filter over the image (m and n don't necessarily have to match the dimensions of the kernel used by the previous layer). The difference is that this time the filter applies a reduce/group function to each of the $m \times n$ sections of the image. Two pooling functions are most commonly used:

- *Max pooling*: Select the maximum/highest value in the underlying subset of the input tensor.

- *Average pooling*: Select the average value in the underlying subset of the input tensor.

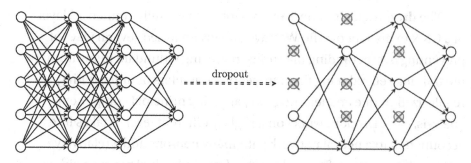

Figure 2-16. *Example of a dropout iteration on a fully connected neural network (Credits: [21])*

An example of how the two operations behave is shown in Figure 2-15. Max pooling is usually preferred over average pooling as it is more effective when it comes to noise reduction—it would only take the value of the highest data point under the filter and discard the others.

The composition of a convolutional layer and a pooling layer is what actually makes a full convolutional layer. You can stack many of these layers in your model, and each layer will detect higher and higher-level features—however, keep in mind that adding more layers also increases the computational demands for training the model. Therefore, the output of a pooling layer can either be attached to another convolutional layer or to a flatten layer ("unwrap" the matrix/tensor into a 1D vector) that will in turn feed it to the fully connected neural network.

2.5.3 Fully connected layer and dropout

The last part of a CNN is the fully connected neural network, exhibiting the same architecture that we have seen previously. It will get the flattened tensor from the convolutional layers as input, and it will have as many units in the output layer as the number of classes that we want the model to identify, with the activation value of each unit expressing the probability for a certain image to belong to a certain class.

145

The **dropout** technique is often applied to the fully connected layer of a CNN to prevent overfit. We have already analyzed several ways of preventing overfit (adding bias units, removing redundant items from the training set, reducing the number of parameters or units, tuning regularization rate and learning rate, applying principal component analysis, etc.). Dropout works on a slightly different level. It takes into account that in a neural network with many neurons and a relatively small training set overfit mostly comes from individual neurons either contributing too much or too little to the final classification, eventually having a detrimental impact on the model's performance. A dropout iteration with parameter p applying during the training phase will remove a certain neuron from the network with probability p and trigger a training iteration without those neurons, as shown in Figure 2-16. By doing so, we force the network to cope with failure without relying on individual neurons (or a set of neurons) for its predictions. Instead, in the absence of some units, the network will rely more on *consensus* among the neurons in a layer.

2.5.4 A network for recognizing images of fruits

Let's move to a practical example of a convolutional neural network for image recognition by picking a dataset a bit more complex than the previous Fashion MNIST. Let's pick, for example, the Fruits 360 dataset from Kaggle [22]—keep in mind, however, that the information reported in this chapter can be used to train a model on any dataset of images.

The Fruits 360 dataset contains about 90,000 images of fruits grouped in 131 classes, each sized 100 × 100 pixels. Download the zip file of the dataset from Kaggle and extract it—in the next examples, I'll assume that the dataset is stored under "/datasets/fruit-360". You'll notice that the dataset has this kind of structure (and you can usually spot a good-quality dataset if it has this kind of structure):

```
fruit-360
   \-> Training
      \-> Apple Braeburn
         \-> image01.jpg
         \-> image02.jpg
         ...
      \-> Apple Crimson Snow
         ...
   \-> Test
      \-> Apple Braeburn
         \-> image01.jpg
         \-> image02.jpg
         ...
      \-> Apple Crimson Snow
         ...
```

We have a directory for the training images and one for the test images, each containing a directory for each class and each class directory containing the images associated to that class. This is usually considered a good practice to structure a dataset of images, and it makes it easy to be used by other developers and applications.

Let's now proceed with importing the modules that we'll need to explore the dataset and train the model:

```python
import os
import numpy as np
import matplotlib.pyplot as plt

from tensorflow.keras import Sequential, layers
from tensorflow.keras.preprocessing.image import
ImageDataGenerator
```

Let's also define a utility function to extract the class names from the dataset:

```
def parse_classes(directory):
    """
    Get the classes of a dataset directory as a vector of
    strings.
    """
        return sorted([
            d for d in os.listdir(directory)
                if os.path.isdir(os.path.join(directory, d))
        ])

classes = parse_classes(train_dir)
```

And a few variables used to define the model:

```
train_dir = os.path.expanduser('~/datasets/fruits-360/
Training')
test_dir = os.path.expanduser('~/datasets/fruits-360/Test')
img_size = (100, 100)
channels = 3      # RGB
epochs = 5        # Number of training epochs
batch_size = 64  # Batch size
```

The batch size is the number of images processed before the model is updated, and it can be tuned to tweak the performance of your model.

A good practice when it comes to image recognition is to use TensorFlow's ImageDataGenerator class on the set of images. The generator will apply several random transformations (rotations, cropping, zoom, etc.) to the input images and generate a new (shuffled) set of images that can be used to make your model more robust when classifying images that, for example, are rotated, cut, blurred, flipped, or zoomed compared to the original images provided in the dataset:

```
train_generator = ImageDataGenerator(rescale=1/255,
    # Rotate the images
    rotation_range=40,
    # Cut the images
    shear_range=0.2,
    # Zoom the images
    zoom_range=0.2,
    # Flip the images
    horizontal_flip=True,
    fill_mode='nearest')

test_generator = ImageDataGenerator(rescale = 1/255)

# Output:
# Found 67692 images belonging to 131 classes.
# Found 22688 images belonging to 131 classes.
```

A few things to note:

- The rescale operation normalizes the images—each pixel has data in the range [0,255], and we want to map it to the range [0, 1].

- It's a good idea to apply all the fancy transformations to the training set, but the test set is usually only rescaled.

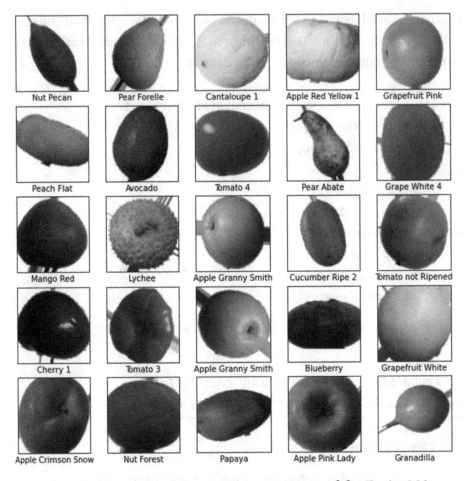

Figure 2-17. *A sample of the training set images of the Fruits 360 dataset*

Let's take a look at how some of these images look like:

```
# Take the first batch of the training set
batch = train_data.next()
# Initialize the plot
plt.figure(figsize=(10,10))
```

```
for i in range(min(25, len(batch[0]))):
    # The first item of batch contains the raw image data
    # The second element contains the labels
    img = batch[0][i]
    label = classes[np.argmax(batch[1][i])]

    plt.subplot(5,5,i+1)
    plt.xticks([])
    plt.yticks([])
    plt.grid(False)
    plt.imshow(img, cmap=plt.cm.binary)
    plt.xlabel(label)

plt.show()
```

The output will probably look something like Figure 2-17.

Now it's time to finally define and compile the model:

```
model = Sequential([
    # First convolutional layer
    layers.Conv2D(filters=32,
        kernel_size=(3,3),
        strides=(1,1),
        padding='valid',
        activation='relu',
        input_shape=(*img_size, channels)
    ),

    # First pooling layer
    layers.MaxPooling2D(pool_size=(2,2)),
```

```python
    # Second convolutional layer
    layers.Conv2D(filters=64,
        kernel_size=(3,3),
        strides=(1,1),
        padding='valid',
        activation='relu',
        input_shape=(*img_size, channels)
    ),

    # Second pooling layer
    layers.MaxPooling2D(pool_size=(2,2)),

    # Flatten output before feeding it to the network
    layers.Flatten(),

    # Neural network input layer
    layers.Dense(units=100, activation='sigmoid'),

    # Link dropout with 15% probability
    layers.Dropout(0.15),

    # Neural network hidden layer
    layers.Dense(units=200, activation='sigmoid'),

    # Link dropout with 15% probability
    layers.Dropout(0.15),

    # Neural network output layer
    layers.Dense(len(classes), activation='softmax')
])

model.compile(loss='categorical_crossentropy',
            optimizer='adam',
            metrics=['accuracy'])
```

In these lines, we have defined a CNN with two pairs of convolutional/pooling layers connected to a fully connected neural network with one input, one hidden, and one output layer. Let's take a closer look at the layers.

First, a convolutional layer is defined as a `Conv2D` object—2D because in this case we are operating on 2D images, but keep in mind that `Conv1D` and `Conv3D` exist as well. `filters` specifies the number of filters to apply to the input—the model will learn which filters extract the most relevant features from the images. If you build a model with multiple convolutional layers, you usually want to increase the number of filters as you go deeper in the network—the filters on the first layer will highlight low-level features (such as edges and luminosity areas), while the layers downstream will use filters that will highlight higher-level features (such as shapes and boundaries).

The `kernel_size` parameter defines the size of the filters to be used—in this case, we'll go for simple 3 × 3 kernels—and `strides` defines how much the filter will be moved over the image on each iteration; we stick to one pixel in the x and y direction. `padding` defines whether the input should be padded—again, `valid` actually means *no padding* (i.e., perform dimensional reduction), while `same` would pad the input to keep the same dimensions on the output. The convolutional layer has an activation function just like the units of the neural layers. `relu` (*rectified linear unit*) is usually the most popular option: given an input x, it simply returns $\max(x,0)$, but sometimes other activation functions may also be used. Finally, we specify the size of each input element as (*width, height, channels*).

The convolutional layer is then connected to the pooling layer—in this case, we use a *max pool* layer. The `pool_size` parameter specifies how large the pool on the input should be—in this case, we use a 2 × 2 pool, which means that each 2 × 2 pixel square on the input will be mapped to one element on the output, therefore reducing the dimensionality by a factor ×4. We then connected another pair of convolutional+pool layers to try and extract even more features from the input, and we then connect the last pooling layer to a Flatten layer which "unwraps" an *n*-dimensional input into a one-dimensional array that can be fed to the input of the fully connected neural network.

We then define the fully connected network using the constructs we explored in the previous example—the output layer has as many units as the number of classes that we want to detect, while you can feel free to experiment with the number of intermediate layers and units to see how it affects the performance. We also introduced two Dropout layers, respectively, between the input and hidden layer and between the hidden and output layer, with *rate* = 0.15—that is, a 15% probability for a connection to a neuron to be cut off during training. Keep in mind that the dropout logic can be very effective in preventing overfit and it helps making the model more robust and less dependent on the contributions of single neurons, but a too high dropout rate will have detrimental effects on its accuracy, since too many of its neurons will be out of use during the training phase. Finally, we compile the model using the categorical_crossentropy loss function (we want to classify items belonging to multiple classes), the adam optimizer, and optimizing for accuracy.

Now that we have defined the CNN, it's time to train it and validate it. When we use an image data generator class, it's possible to group together training and validation through the fit_generator method instead of the usual fit:

```
history = model.fit(
    train_data,
    steps_per_epoch=train_data.samples/batch_size,
    validation_data=test_data,
    validation_steps=test_data.samples/batch_size,
    epochs=epochs
)
```

Time to go and make yourself a coffee or a tea—since we are training a model with more layers and way more images than our previous vanilla neural network trained on the Fashion MNIST, this phase may take between 30 and 90 minutes to complete depending on the power of the machine:

```
Epoch 1/5
loss: 2.6444 - accuracy: 0.3622 - val_loss: 1.5080 - val_
accuracy: 0.7355
Epoch 2/5
loss: 0.7892 - accuracy: 0.8084 - val_loss: 0.9297 - val_
accuracy: 0.8696
Epoch 3/5
loss: 0.3591 - accuracy: 0.9142 - val_loss: 0.2119 - val_
accuracy: 0.9212
Epoch 4/5
loss: 0.2093 - accuracy: 0.9474 - val_loss: 0.0216 - val_
accuracy: 0.9448
Epoch 5/5
loss: 0.1590 - accuracy: 0.9570 - val_loss: 0.0087 - val_
accuracy: 0.9573
```

The resulting accuracy history is shown in Figure 2-18.

We can then proceed with analyzing the progress of the accuracy over the training epochs.

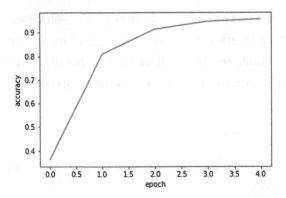

Figure 2-18. *Progress in the accuracy of the model over 5 epochs*

```
epochs = history.epoch
accuracy = history.history['accuracy']

fig = plt.figure()
plot = fig.add_subplot()
plot.set_xlabel('epoch')
plot.set_ylabel('accuracy')
plot.plot(epochs, accuracy)
```

You'll notice a very high accuracy (>95%) both on the training and test set, much higher than our previous examples that involved either simple regression or vanilla neural networks. This is a quite impressive achievement considering that this time we have 131 possible output classes, and it shows how adding one or more convolutional layers to a neural network and leveraging mechanisms such as dropout to prevent overfit can effectively increase the performance of a model. You can also use the `evaluate` function to estimate the performance of the model on the test set, as done in the previous examples, since it also supports generators:

```
model.evaluate(test_data)
```

Finally, we can use the model to make simple predictions—we can, for example, take some image from the test set:

```
test_batch = test_data.next()
test_images = test_batch[0]
test_labels = test_batch[1]

test_img = test_images[0]
expected_class = classes[np.argmax(test_labels[0])]
predicted_class = classes[np.argmax(model.predict(
np.asarray([test_img])))]
print(f'Expected class: {expected_class}.\n' +
    f'Predicted class: {predicted_class}')
```

And we can also run the model on a few images from the test set and plot them with their expected and predicted classes and the confidence levels of the predictions using the plot_results function defined in the previous examples:

```
plot_results(
    images=test_images,
    labels=[np.argmax(label_values) for label_values in test_
    labels],
    classes=classes,
    predictions=predictions,
    rows=6, cols=3
)
```

You will probably see a figure like the one shown in Figure 2-19. As a last step, don't forget to save your model (using the model_save function we have defined in the previous examples); otherwise, you'll have to go through the whole training phase again!

You should now have all the basic tools to train a neural network for image recognition, and we can shift the focus from how to build a neural network on some sample datasets to how to collect images to be used in our own applications.

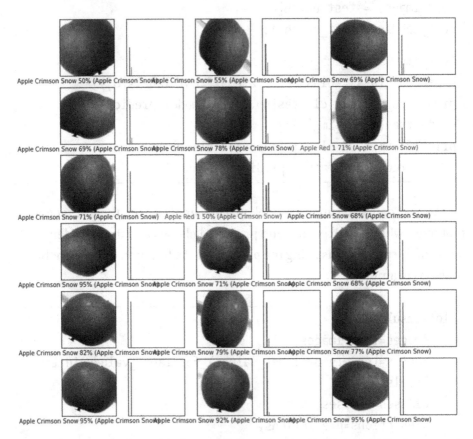

Figure 2-19. *Evaluating the model against a few images in the test set*

CHAPTER 3

Computer Vision on Raspberry Pi

Now that we have a good understanding of how to build a machine learning model with TensorFlow, it's time to put our knowledge into practice and train a model that can recognize the presence of people in a room and can run on a Raspberry Pi with some cheap hardware.

The Raspberry Pi is arguably the most successful credit card–sized system-on-chip (SoC) developed in the past decade. Its compact form factor, flexibility, and affordable price (the price goes from about $10 for the tiny single-core Raspberry Pi Zero up to about $80 for a quad-core Raspberry Pi 4 with 8GB of RAM) have made it a very attractive option for many IoT projects. It's definitely not a power horse when it comes to machine learning applications (if you are looking for a more beefed embedded machine to train more complex models, you may want to opt for solutions such as the NVIDIA Jetson boards), and my suggestion is usually to train your model on your laptop or a more powerful machine, but once you have trained a not-too-complex model, the Raspberry Pi can definitely be a good candidate to run predictions. Note, however, that the least powerful options (such as the Raspberry Pi Zero and the Raspberry Pi A+) may experience a bit of latency when it comes to run TensorFlow code, but I have run many models on Raspberry Pi 3 and 4 devices, and, as long as the models aren't too complex, I haven't encountered any issues.

© Fabio Manganiello 2021
F. Manganiello, *Computer Vision with Maker Tech*,
https://doi.org/10.1007/978-1-4842-6821-6_3

In this chapter, we'll see how to use a Raspberry Pi and a cheap infrared camera to build a real-time model to recognize the presence of people in a room. While many of the examples explored in the previous chapters involved models trained on "normal" images from optical cameras, detecting the presence of people in a small environment is, in my experience, a task better performed by infrared cameras. If you think of that, there can be many ways people may be standing or sitting in a room, and you may have a different number of people in the room as well, at an arbitrary distance from your camera, in arbitrary conditions of luminosity. That makes the task of building a robust model for presence detection on optical images quite challenging—the model will have to be trained on a vast dataset representing as much as possible all the variability of the real environment, and it will likely have many layers to discern all the possible patterns, making it prone to overfit. Infrared cameras are much better suited for this task. Since an infrared camera detects changes in the gradient of temperature of any objects in front of it, it's not sensitive to changes in luminosity conditions, neither it is sensitive to changes in the position of the person. The only issue I have experienced with this approach is when the environment is too warm—an infrared camera is a very good tool to detect people if the temperature of the bodies is around 36–37°C and the environment is cooler, but if the environment is around the same temperature as a human body, then the gradient temperature isn't sufficient to detect the presence of people—but if the temperature of your room is usually below 36 degrees, then you can go on with this approach! However, as a follow-up, you can also easily adapt the process illustrated in this chapter to an application with optical images—it may require a larger dataset, a longer training phase, and a CNN with more layers, but the process is exactly the same. The process illustrated in this chapter can easily be extended to any application that requires data gathering, labelling, training a model, and deploying that model for real-time predictions.

This project consists of four phases:

1. Prepare the hardware and software.

2. Build the logic that captures snapshots from the infrared camera at regular intervals, normalizes them, and stores them somewhere.

3. Label the pictures (presence detected/no presence detected) and train a model on them.

4. Deploy the model on the Raspberry Pi and run it periodically against newly captured images to detect the presence of people in the room. Optionally, we may add some additional logic that runs some pieces of automation when the model runs (e.g., turn the lights on/off when someone enters/exits the room, or get a mobile notification if presence is detected but we are not at home).

3.1 Preparing the hardware and the software

The examples in this chapter have been extensively tested on Raspberry Pi, but they should work fine with little or no modifications on any Linux-based SoC.

3.1.1 Preparing the hardware

You can use any Raspberry Pi [23] device to capture images, deploy your model, and use it to make predictions. However, as mentioned previously, low-power devices such as the Raspberry Pi Zero may experience more latency—even though I have successfully deployed the people detection model to a Raspberry Pi Zero, I couldn't get anything below 2–3 seconds of base latency when it comes to capturing images or making predictions. Any Raspberry Pi 3 or higher, however, should provide fluid performance for basic machine learning projects.

So, in order to get started, you'll need

1. A Raspberry Pi or any similar Linux-based SoC.

2. An empty micro SD card (preferably 16GB or more). It's also a good idea to check the quality and speed of your SD card—ultra-fast SanDisk cards are, in my experience, a good pick to flash the Raspberry Pi operating system, but anything fast enough and robust enough should do the job.

3. An infrared camera. The examples in this chapter will be based on the Pimoroni MLX90640-based thermal camera breakout [24] (see Figure 3-1), a relatively cheap 24x32 thermal camera that does a good job in capturing thermal gradients with a depth of a few meters, but any thermal or infrared camera should work.

Figure 3-1. *Pimoroni MLX90640 thermal camera breakout*

A few words on the hardware protocol if you use an MLX90640 breakout camera or any camera other than a USB camera or the native PiCamera. This breakout works over I^2C protocol. When it comes to electronics for Raspberry Pi, Arduino, and other IoT devices, you may usually find three popular hardware protocols:

1. I^2C

2. SPI (Serial Peripheral Interface)

3. Direct GPIO

Direct GPIO basically means a direct mapping between the pinout of your device and the master (Raspberry Pi, Arduino, ESP, etc.). It is usually a popular option for simple devices with a low number of pins and transmission rate, while devices with higher throughput usually opt for a bus-based interface—I^2C and SPI are usually the most popular protocols in this space. A high-level comparison between these two bus interfaces is shown in Figure 3-2. I^2C was originally developed in 1982 by Philips Semiconductors, and it's been around for long enough to be widely used by many hardware devices. It is a synchronous, bidirectional, packet-based serial communication protocol that relies on two connectors present on each device:

1. SDA (Serial Data Line), used to transfer data in both directions over a serial bus interface

2. SCL (Serial Clock Line), used to synchronize the connected devices and regulate access to the bus

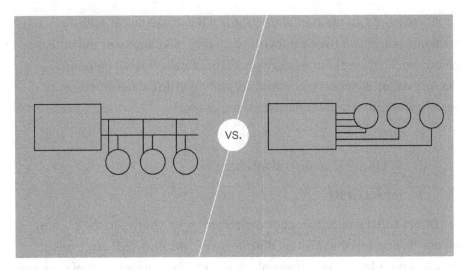

Figure 3-2. *Comparison between the physical bus connections of I²C (left) and SPI (right) (Credits: Lifewire)*

The MLX90640 uses this interface, and therefore, it includes both an SDA and SCL connector, which can be connected to the *I²C* interface of the Raspberry Pi (or any SoC with compatible pinout). The VCC and GND connectors will have to be connected to the same power source and ground line as the Raspberry Pi or any of the Raspberry Pi 3.3V/GND pins, while we can omit the INT (interrupt) connection in this project, which is usually used to raise asynchronous events. There are mainly three options to connect an *I²C* or SPI device to a Raspberry Pi:

1. Hardware *I²C* connection. Even though the GPIO pins of a Raspberry Pi are supposed to be general-purpose (as the name itself suggests), some pins are optimized on hardware level to better operate some purposes over others. That's the case for the GPIO pins 2 and 3, which, as shown in Figure 3-3, are configured to act, respectively, as SDA and SCL interfaces. The quickest option is therefore to connect the SDA and SCL pins of your *I²C* camera

directly to these pins. The advantage of this type of connection is that it is fast (since it uses the native hardware implementation of the I^2C protocol) and it requires nearly no software configuration to work. The disadvantage is that a Raspberry Pi only sports a pair of specialized SDA/SCL pins, and you can only connect one device to this interface (it's not a big problem if you only use the Raspberry Pi GPIO for the thermal camera, but it could be an issue if you want to connect more I^2C devices).

2. Software I^2C connection. In this configuration, you can use any GPIO pair of pins as a SDA/SCL interface. The advantage of this approach is that you have much more flexibility to connect more I^2C devices, or, more generally, you can connect more devices without necessarily occupying the GPIO pins 2 and 3. The disadvantages of this approach are represented by its speed (the protocol is managed by the software, specifically by the kernel, which is usually slower than a hardware-based implementation) and the fact that it may require a bit more tuning of the software configuration.

3. Use a breakout board like the *Breakout Garden* [25] (see Figure 3-4). This is probably my favorite approach. Breakout boards can be plugged directly on top of your Raspberry Pi GPIO pins, and they act as a hardware multiplexer for I^2C and SPI devices. They provide a hardware interface to connect up to four I^2C devices and two SPI devices, and they make the connection as easy as physically plugging the device into the slot—no wiring nor soldering required.

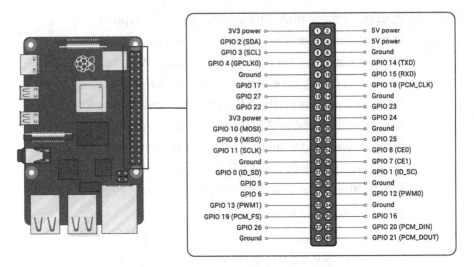

Figure 3-3. Raspberry Pi GPIO (Credits: Raspberry Pi Foundation)

3.1.2 Preparing the operating system

Once you've got all the hardware in place, it's time to flash the operating system of your Raspberry Pi on the SD card. The most popular options are usually NOOBS [26], a Debian-based distribution easy to use also for those who aren't particularly fluent with a terminal, and Raspberry Pi OS [27] (formerly Raspbian), a more general-purpose Debian-based distribution for Raspberry Pi. As a strong supporter of Arch Linux, most of the examples have been intensively tested on devices running Arch Linux ARM, but since the learning curve to get Arch to run on an embedded device is usually higher than getting NOOBS or Raspberry Pi OS, the examples in this chapter will mainly target these two distributions. They should, however, work with minor or no modifications on any other Raspberry Pi operating system—the only differences may be in the way you install some system packages, for example, through "pacman" or "yum" instead of "apt-get".

Download the image of Raspberry Pi OS or NOOBS for your device and flash it to the SD card. You can use any software to write the image—the Raspberry Pi Foundation provides an *Imager* program for Windows and macOS to write the image, but you can find many of them with a web search. If you are on Linux, you can easily write the image using the built-in dd command:

```
# FIRST check where your SD card is mounted!!
# Make sure that you don't write the image to any other hard
drive!
cat /proc/partitions  # Find something like e.g. /dev/sdb

[sudo] dd if=/path/to/raspberrypi-os-version.img of=/dev/sdb \
    conv=fsync bs=4M status=progress
```

Once the image is flashed, (safely) remove the SD card from your computer and plug it into the Raspberry Pi. At least for the first boot it's advised to also plug a monitor (over HDMI) and a USB keyboard/mouse. Once everything is connected, plug in the USB power source and boot the Raspberry Pi. After a few seconds, you should see a welcome screen on the connected display. If any login is required, the default credentials are **user=pi** and **password=raspberry**. Other systems may have different default credentials—please consult their web page if that's the case. It is a **very** good practice, however, to change the default credentials as soon as you can, especially if you are planning to enable remote SSH access—just open a terminal and type *passwd*.

Figure 3-4. *A Breakout Garden I²C/SPI hardware multiplexer (Credits: Pimoroni)*

If your Raspberry Pi is connected over a network cable, then it will probably connect to the network by itself without any configuration. Otherwise, if you are planning to connect it over Wi-Fi, it's a good idea to enable the interface now—you can do it either from the Wi-Fi icon in the application panel or through the terminal (`raspi-config` command). Other options include manually creating and enabling a `netctl` profile or using another network manager.

Once the Raspberry Pi is connected, it's a good idea to enable SSH (and, optionally, VNC) so you can easily access it from your laptop without an attached screen and mouse/keyboard. Use `raspi-config` to enable the SSH service or manually start and enable the `sshd` service:

```
[sudo] systemctl start sshd.service
[sudo] systemctl enable sshd.service
```

Take note of the IP address of the device (`ifconfig` or `ip addr`), head back to your computer, and use PuTTY or the command-line ssh client to connect to your Raspberry Pi:

```
ssh pi@[ip-of-the-rpi]
```

Once you are logged in, it's time to install the software dependencies to get our project to run.

3.2 Installing the software dependencies

The examples in this chapter will use Platypush [28] as a platform to automatically capture images, run the model, and perform automation routines. I have built Platypush myself over the past years, and it is now mature enough to perform many tasks on a SoC device. However, it should be relatively easy to port the examples in this chapter to other common automation platform as well—such as Home Assistant or OpenHAB.

First, check the version of Python on the Raspberry Pi through `python3 -version`—you'll need at least the version 3.6 or higher to run Platypush. That shouldn't be a problem on most of the modern distributions, but older distributions may have older versions—if that's the case, either upgrade the distribution or compile a higher version of Python manually.

Time to update the apt mirrors to see if there are any package updates:

```
[sudo] apt-get update
[sudo] apt-get upgrade
```

Then install `pip` if it's not installed already:

```
[sudo] apt-get install python3-pip
```

And then install Platypush—for now with the http module. There are two ways to do it:

1. Install the latest stable version via pip:

```
[sudo] pip3 install 'platypush[http]'
```

2. Install the latest snapshot from GitHub. This approach is particularly advised if you are planning to use the MLX90640 breakout or any other devices that require specific drivers that need to be compiled from the Platypush codebase. First make sure that git is installed:

```
[sudo] apt-get install git
```

Then clone the repository and its submodules:

```
mkdir -p ~/projects && cd ~/projects
git clone https://github.com/BlackLight/platypush
cd platypush
git submodule init
git submodule update

[sudo] pip3 install '.[http]'
```

Also, Platypush relies on Redis as a messaging system to dispatch commands between different components. Install, start, and enable Redis on the Raspberry Pi:

```
# On other systems the Redis server is called simply redis
[sudo] apt-get install redis-server
[sudo] systemctl start redis-server.service
[sudo] systemctl enable redis-server.service
```

It's now time to take a look at the Platypush modules we need for our purposes. Platypush comes with an extensive set of integrations documented on the official documentation page [29], each of them may require different dependencies or its own configuration. By default, the configuration is read from ~/.config/platypush/config.yaml; each module can be configured in this file (in YAML format) by using the same attributes shown in the constructor parameters (also, it is **strongly** advised to run Platypush as a non-root user). Modules can be divided into *plugins* and *backends*. Plugins are (usually) stateless and can be used to perform actions—such as turn on the lights, play the music, capture a camera frame, make predictions from a model, and so on. Backends are instead services that run in the background and trigger *events* when something happens (e.g., some media file is played, an email is received, a calendar event is created, some data is read from a sensor, etc.)—although some plugins may also raise events. These events can be caught by custom event *hooks* that can run any piece of logic you like. Some modules require extra dependencies—they are usually reported in the documentation of the module and can usually be installed via pip. The dependencies are also reported in the project's requirements.txt—you can uncomment the ones you need and then install them through

```
[sudo] pip3 install -r requirements.txt
```

The dependencies are also reported in the project's setup.py file, and they can be installed via

```
[sudo] pip3 install 'platypush[module1,module2,module3]'
```

For the purposes of this project, we'd like to first capture images at regular intervals from our camera and store them locally so we can use them later to train our model. If you are using the MLX90640 thermal camera breakout, then you'll first have to compile the driver provided by Pimoroni. First, install the required dependencies:

```
[sudo] apt-get install libi2c-dev build-essentials
```

Then move to the Platypush repository directory you have previously cloned and compile the driver:

```
cd ~/projects/platypush/plugins/camera/ir/mlx90640/lib
make clean
make bcm2835
make examples/rawrgb I2C_MODE=LINUX
```

If the compilation process goes fine, you should find an executable file named rawrgb under the folder examples. Take note of the path of this executable or copy it to another bin directory. If you try to run it and the MLX90640 breakout is properly connected, you should see a continuous flow of bytes—that's the RGB representation of the frames captured by the camera. If something goes wrong, it's usually because the I^2C bus is not enabled on the Raspberry Pi. If that's the case, you can enable the I^2C interface either through raspi-config or by manually adding this line to /boot/config.txt:

```
dtparam=i2c_arm=on
# Optionally, increase the throughput on the bus
dtparam=i2c1_baudrate=400000
```

Note that on some systems the dtparam may be named i2c instead of i2c_arm, and changing the I^2C configuration may require a system restart. Once the rawrgb executable can successfully capture frames, install the Platypush generic camera module dependencies:

```
cd ~/projects/platypush
[sudo] pip3 install '.[camera]'
# Or, if you installed Platypush directly from pip:
[sudo] pip3 install 'platypush[camera]'
```

If you opted for a camera that can be connected over the hardware Raspberry Pi camera interface, you should install the picamera module instead (and also make sure that the PiCamera interface is enabled in raspi-config):

```
cd ~/projects/platypush
[sudo] pip3 install '.[picamera]'
# Or, if you installed Platypush directly from pip:
[sudo] pip3 install 'platypush[picamera]'
```

If instead you have a USB-connected camera, you may connect Platypush to it through the camera.cv, camera.ffmpeg, or camera. gstreamer plugins, which, respectively, interact with a camera device over OpenCV, FFmpeg, and GStreamer (check their documentation pages or setup.py for their required dependencies). The camera interface provided

173

by Platypush offers an API to transparently interact with any of these plugins. Once all the dependencies are installed, you can proceed with configuring the Platypush automation.

First, enable the web server in Platypush—we'll be using it both for accessing the camera from the web interface and test capturing over the web API. Add these lines to ~/.config/platypush/config.yaml:

```
backend.http:
    port: 8008  # Default listen port
```

Secondly, we'll configure the camera.ir.mlx90640 plugin and specify where the rawrgb path is:

```
camera.ir.mlx90640:
    rawrgb_path: ~/bin/rawrgb
    # You may want to specify the rotation of the camera
    rotate: 270
    # Optionally, specify the number of frames per second
    fps: 16
    # And flip the image vertically/horizontally
    vertical_flip: True
    horizontal_flip: True
```

If instead you opted for collecting images through a PiCamera-compatible optical or infrared camera, the configuration will look something like this:

```
camera.pi:
    # Same options as camera.ir.mlx90640
    # except it doesn't need the rawrgb_path
```

Or, in the case of a camera compatible with OpenCV/FFmpeg/GStreamer:

```
camera.cv:
    device: /dev/video0
    # Same options available for camera.pi

camera.ffmpeg:
    device: /dev/video0
    # Same options available for camera.pi

camera.gstreamer:
    device: /dev/video0
    # Same options available for camera.pi
```

Now you can start the service through the platypush command. It's also a good idea to register it as a user service, so you won't have to manually restart it on each reboot or if it terminates:

```
mkdir -p ~/.config/systemd/user
cd ~/projects/platypush
cp examples/systemd/platypush.service ~/.config/systemd/user
# You may also want to modify the ExecStart parameter if
# Platypush was installed on a path other than /usr/bin
systemctl --user daemon-reload
systemctl --user start platypush.service
systemctl --user enable platypush.service
```

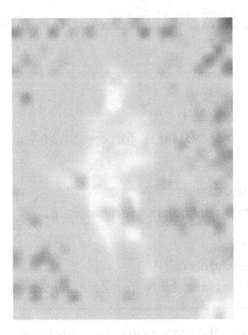

Figure 3-5. *A snapshot from the MLX90640 infrared camera*

If Platypush started successfully, you can check that the web panel is accessible from a browser at `http://raspberry-pi-ip:8008/`. On the first access, you will be required to set a username and password. Upon login, you can select the panel associated to the infrared camera (it's usually identified by a sun-shaped icon) and start streaming.

If all went smooth, you should see a stream of images as shown in Figures 3-5 and 3-6, showing green-blue areas where a colder temperature is detected and yellow-red where the temperature is higher. If instead you used another camera plugin (`camera.pi`, `camera.cv`, `camera.ffmpeg`, or `camera.gstreamer`), you should also see its interface in the tab, and the following instructions will work regardless of the camera interface you used—you'll just have to replace `camera.ir.mlx90640` with the name of the camera plugin you used.

You can also capture single images by directly opening the capture URL:

```
http://raspberry-pi-ip:8008/camera/ir.mlx90640/photo?scale_
x=10&scale_y=10
```

The scale_x and scale_y parameters may be needed to boost the resolution of the images, as the MLX90640 captures images at a small 24x32 resolution. If you want to access the continuous stream instead, just replace photo in the preceding URL with video, and replace camera/ir.mlx90640 with, for example, camera.pi or camera.cv if you use a different plugin.

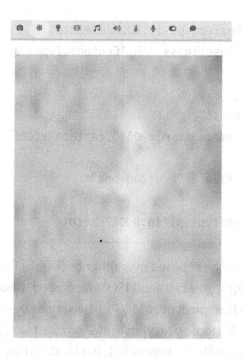

Figure 3-6. *Preview of the web panel MLX90640 interface*

Platypush exposes its API over HTTP as well, and you can use it to programmatically take pictures or record video streams from the camera, for example:

```
curl -XPOST -u 'user:pass' -H 'Content-Type: application/
json' -d '
{
    "type":"request",
    "action":"camera.ir.mlx90640.capture_image",
    "args": {
        "image_file": "~/image.jpg"
    }
}' http://raspberrypi-pi-ip:8008/execute
curl -XPOST -u 'user:pass' -H 'Content-Type: application/
json' -d '
{
    "type":"request",
    "action":"camera.ir.mlx90640.capture_video",
    "args": {
        "video_file": "~/video.mp4"
    }
}' http://raspberrypi-pi-ip:8008/execute
```

This API can also be exposed over other backends. For example, if you enable backend.mqtt, you can send JSON-formatted messages like the preceding ones to Platypush over MQTT (the service by default will listen for commands on the topic platypush_bus_mq/hostname), and a similar principle applies to backend.websocket, backend.kafka, and backend. redis. So keep in mind that you have multiple interfaces to run your commands, in case you prefer not to expose a web service.

The API is also available for other camera plugins—just replace `camera.ir.mlx90640` with the name of your camera plugin. In general, any method shown in the plugin documentation can be called over the HTTP API.

3.3 Capturing the images

Now that we've got all the hardware and software in place, let's configure Platypush to periodically capture camera images at regular intervals and store them locally—we'll later use these images to train our model.

Platypush provides the concept of cronjobs, which are basically procedures that can be executed at regular intervals and run some custom actions. Let's add a cron to our `config.yaml` that takes pictures from the sensor and stores them in a local directory. First, create the images directory on the Raspberry Pi:

```
mkdir -p ~/datasets/people_detect
```

Then add the logic for the cron in the `config.yaml`:

```
cron.ThermalCameraSnapshotCron:
  cron_expression: '* * * * *'
  actions:
    - action: camera.ir.mlx90640.capture_image
      args:
        image_file: ~/datasets/people_detect/\
          ${int(__import__('time').time())}.jpg
        grayscale: true
```

A few observations:

- Platypush cronjobs are identified by the `cron.<CRON_NAME>` syntax.

- The `cron_expression` defines how often the cron should be executed. It's the same syntax as a UNIX cronjob, so in this case, `* * * * *` means *take a picture once a minute*. Seconds are also supported for higher granularity, but for back compatibility with the UNIX cron expressions, they are usually reported at the end of the expression—so if you wanted to run the procedure every 30 seconds, the expression would be `* * * * * */30`.

- The actions to be executed are defined in the `actions` section as a list.

- Each `action` has a `<plugin_name>.<method_name>` syntax and optionally an `args` attribute to specify its arguments. The list of actions available for a certain plugin is reported in the documentation of the plugin itself, together with the list of supported arguments.

- You can embed snippets of Python in the definition of a Platypush cron, procedure, or event hook using the `${}` syntax. In this case, we are using the `~/datasets/people_detect/${int(__import__('time').time())}.jpg` argument to save each image under our dataset directory as a timestamp-named file.

- When it comes to infrared/thermal pictures, I have experienced the best performance by converting the RGB output to grayscale—the Platypush plugin for the MLX90640 has already a built-in logic that converts

RGB thermal pictures to grayscale by assigning more weight to the red components and subtracting the contribution of the blue components. A grayscale conversion with properly assigned weights for the color components makes it very easy to generate images that clearly show warm areas in white and cold areas in black—and that can make a machine learning model converge very quickly. If you use different infrared or thermal cameras that also output RGB artifacts, check their temperature range and sensitivity to understand how to leverage the output color space to boost the temperature range that you want to detect when converting to grayscale.

- Again, the cron would work with little modifications with any other camera plugin—simply replace `camera.ir.mlx90640` with the plugin you want to use, and as long as it implements the abstract `camera` interface, it will work fine with the same API.

After defining the camera capture logic, (re)start Platypush and wait until the tick of the next minute. If everything went fine, the first grayscale thermal picture should have been stored under `~/datasets/people_detect`. Leave the logic running for at least 1–2 days to capture enough pictures—in my experience, the model could already perform well when trained with ~900–1000 images. Try to enrich the dataset as much as possible—it is sufficient to walk around the room, stand at different points of the room, capture images when more people are in the room, take pictures while you are far from the sensor, and so on. The higher the variability of the conditions captured in the training set, the more accurate the model will behave in real-world scenarios. Also, make sure that you have a balanced number of pictures with and without people in front of the sensor—ideally, aim at a 50/50 split.

3.4 Labelling the images

Once you have captured enough images, it's time to copy them over to your computer to label them and train the model. If you have followed the instructions reported earlier in the chapter and have enabled SSH on the Raspberry Pi (and you have an SSH server running either on the Raspberry Pi or on your main computer), this will be as simple as running this command on your Raspberry Pi:

```
scp -r ~/datasets user@your-pc:/home/user/
```

The boring part awaits us now—manually labelling the images as positive or negative. I have made this task a bit less tedious with a script that allows you to interactively label the images while you view them, and it moves them to the right target directory. Install the dependency and clone the repository on your local computer:

```
# The script uses OpenCV as a cross-platform
# tool to display images.
[sudo] pip3 install opencv

# Create a folder for the image utils and
# clone the repository
mkdir -p ~/projects
cd ~/projects
git clone https://github.com/BlackLight/imgdetect-utils
```

The labelling script will look for image files in a directory and will consider any sub-directory as a label. Let's proceed with creating our labels and start the labelling process:

```
UTILS_DIR=~/projects/imgdetect-utils
IMG_DIR=~/datasets/people_detect

# Create the directories for the labels
cd $IMG_DIR
mkdir -p positive negative

# Do the labelling
cd $UTILS_DIR
python3 utils/label.py -d "$IMG_DIR" --scale-factor 10
```

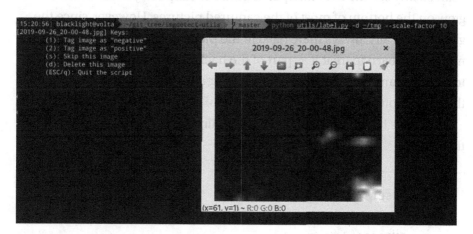

Figure 3-7. *Screenshot of the image labelling phase through the* utils/label.py *script*

You should see a window like the one shown in Figure 3-7. You can use the number keys (1 for negative, 2 for positive in this case) to label a certain image as positive or negative, s to skip an image, d to delete it, and ESC/q to terminate the labelling. The –scale-factor 10 passed to the script tells to scale up the images by a factor of 10 when previewing—that's quite useful when we label tiny 24x32 images. Let the timestamps guide you (e.g., to understand when people were in the room and when not), and keep in mind that lighter areas represent warmer bodies, while darker areas represent colder bodies or the background, so you are likely to see human bodies in the pictures as "white halos," whose size and brightness depends on how distant they are from the sensor and in which position they are. Keep also in mind that other sources of heat can pop up in the images if they are within the range of the camera sensor—something to keep in mind if you have kettles, boilers, or simply pets walking around the room— but they shouldn't be a big issue if they are part of the "background" and they are there in most of the pictures. For example, my MLX90640 sits in a Breakout Garden just on top of a Raspberry Pi 4 with active cooling, and I can clearly see the heat dissipated from the Raspberry Pi fan as a light glow on the bottom of most of the captured pictures. However, since the glow is basically always there (also in the pictures labelled as negative), the model will learn to treat it as part of the background and it's not expected to trigger many false positives. However, keep in mind that this may not be the case if you have a cat walking in front of the sensor every now and then.

After the labelling phase, the dataset directory will look something like this:

```
-> ~/datasets/people_detect
  -> negative
    -> IMG0001.jpg
    -> IMG0002.jpg
    ...
  -> positive
    -> IMG0003.jpg
    -> IMG0004.jpg
    ...
```

Once you are done with the labelling process, you should have the two directories in your dataset (positive and negative) properly populated with your training images, and you are ready to proceed with the next phase—training the model to detect the presence of people.

3.5 Training the model

This part should be quite straightforward if you apply the same techniques explored in the previous chapters. We have a neatly labelled dataset of 24x32 grayscale thermal camera pictures stored under ~/datasets/people_detect, and we want to train a neural network that learns when an image contains a human figure and when it doesn't—so it's time to open a new Jupyter notebook.

Let's start with defining a few variables:

```
import os

# Define the dataset directories
datasets_dir = os.path.join(os.path.expanduser('~'),
'datasets')
dataset_dir = os.path.join(datasets_dir, 'people_detect')

# Define the size of the input images. In the case of an
# MLX90640 it will be (24, 32) for horizontal images and
# (32, 24) for vertical images
image_size = (32, 24)

# Image generator batch size
batch_size = 64

# Number of training epochs
epochs = 5
```

In this case, the data is not already neatly split into training set and test set like in some of the previous examples, but we can leverage the validation_split parameter of the Keras ImageDataGenerator class to let it automatically split the dataset into training and test set—the split value in particular will tell the constructor which percentage of the data points should go into the test/validation set. We can then use the subset argument of flow_from_directory to extract the two sets.

```python
from tensorflow.keras.preprocessing.image import
ImageDataGenerator

# 30% of the images goes into the test set
generator = ImageDataGenerator(rescale=1./255, validation_
split=0.3)

train_data = generator.flow_from_directory(dataset_dir,
                                           target_size=image_
                                           size,
                                           batch_size=batch_
                                           size,
                                           subset='training',
                                           class_mode=
                                           'categorical',
                                           color_
                                           mode='grayscale')

test_data = generator.flow_from_directory(dataset_dir,
                                          target_size=image_
                                          size,
                                          batch_size=batch_
                                          size,
                                          subset='validation',
```

```
                                          class_mode=
                                          'categorical',
                                          color_mode=
                                          'grayscale')
```

Unlike the example in the previous chapter, here we are assuming that your Raspberry Pi and the camera won't move much, if you are going to monitor for presence of people within the same room, so the snapshots are expected to always capture the same view and therefore we won't need much image transformation—the only transformation performed by the image generator is the 1/255 rescale to normalize the image pixel values within the [0, 1] range. If instead you expect to move the camera around or to install it on top of some moving components, it's still a good idea to add transformations such as horizontal_flip, vertical_flip, rotate, and so on to the image generator to create a more robust dataset. Also, since we are dealing with grayscale images, we need to specify the right color space to flow_from_directory through the color_mode argument. Like in the previous examples, let's take a peek at the dataset to see if everything looks alright:

```
import numpy as np
import matplotlib.pyplot as plt

index_to_label = {
    index: label
    for label, index in train_data.class_indices.items()
}

plt.figure(figsize=(10, 10))
batch = train_data.next()
```

```
for i in range(min(25, len(batch[0]))):
    img = batch[0][i]
    label = index_to_label[np.argmax(batch[1][i])]
    plt.subplot(5, 5, i+1)
    plt.xticks([])
    plt.yticks([])
    plt.grid(False)

    # Note the np.squeeze call - matplotlib can't
    # process grayscale images unless the extra
    # 1-sized dimension is removed.
    plt.imshow(np.squeeze(img))
    plt.xlabel(label)

plt.show()
```

You should see a figure like the one shown in Figure 3-8.

Time to define and train the model. The model for this example can be quite simple and yet achieve impressive accuracy, if you train it with enough images. For example, let's define a model that flattens the 32 × 24 grayscale images, which includes two hidden layers with a number of units that is, respectively, 80% and 30% the number of input pixels, and outputs the predictions on an output layer of two units—negative and positive:

```
import tensorflow as tf
from tensorflow import keras

model = keras.Sequential([
    keras.layers.Flatten(input_shape=image_size),
    keras.layers.Dense(round(0.8 * image_size[0] *
    image_size[1]),
        activation=tf.nn.relu),
```

```
    keras.layers.Dense(round(0.3 * image_size[0] * image_
    size[1]),
        activation=tf.nn.relu),
    keras.layers.Dense(len(train_data.class_indices),
        activation=tf.nn.softmax)
])

model.compile(loss='categorical_crossentropy',
            optimizer='adam',
            metrics=['accuracy'])
```

Let's train it over the previously declared data generator:

```
history = model.fit(
    train_data,
    steps_per_epoch=train_data.samples/batch_size,
    validation_data=test_data,
    validation_steps=test_data.samples/batch_size,
    epochs=epochs
)
```

The output on my system looks like this:

```
Epoch 1/5
loss: 0.2529 - accuracy: 0.9196 - val_loss: 0.0543 - val_
accuracy: 0.9834
Epoch 2/5
loss: 0.0572 - accuracy: 0.9801 - val_loss: 0.0213 - val_
accuracy: 0.9967
Epoch 3/5
loss: 0.0254 - accuracy: 0.9915 - val_loss: 0.0080 - val_
accuracy: 1.0000
```

```
Epoch 4/5
loss: 0.0117 - accuracy: 0.9979 - val_loss: 0.0053 - val_
accuracy: 0.9967
Epoch 5/5
loss: 0.0058 - accuracy: 1.0000 - val_loss: 0.0046 - val_
accuracy: 0.9983
```

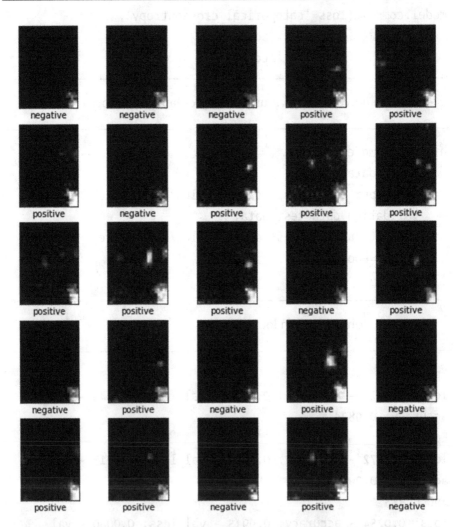

Figure 3-8. *A preview of some of the items in the training set*

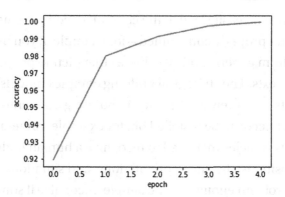

Figure 3-9. *Accuracy of the thermal camera people detection model over 5 training epochs*

It means a 100% accuracy on the training set and 99.83% accuracy over the test set after 5 epochs—not bad at all considering that we have used a relatively simple network with no convolutional layers. Like in the previous examples, we can visualize how the accuracy of the model improved over the training epochs:

```
epochs = history.epoch
accuracy = history.history['accuracy']

fig = plt.figure()
plot = fig.add_subplot()
plot.set_xlabel('epoch')
plot.set_ylabel('accuracy')
plot.plot(epochs, accuracy)
```

You should see a plot like the one shown in Figure 3-9.

The reason for such high performance despite the relatively small dataset (I have used a dataset of about 1400 images for these examples) and simple network architecture is that we have used the right tools to solve the problem before even building the model. The problem of people detection can easily lead to the creation of complex models if the problem isn't properly constrained—for example, if you use generic large datasets from generic optical cameras that picture people in tons of different contexts. The strategy of building complex models from large generic datasets can surely work if you are building a general-purpose application that needs to be installed on, for example, camera hardware for autonomous vehicles that need to recognize a human body in all the possible positions, distances, orientations, and situations. But if you constrain the problem enough—for example, recognize if somebody is present in your room, from a static camera that doesn't move, that detects temperature gradients instead of relying on the light that bounces on a body, in a color space that is optimized for the purpose, and with an input source that generally produces very similar images in the case of negatives—then the model doesn't necessarily have to be complex, and the dataset doesn't necessarily have to be huge. That's because we have translated the problem of *detect the presence of people in a picture* into a problem of *detect the presence of more light halos than usual in a grayscale picture*. In most of the cases, defining a good input source, input space, and input dataset is the most important ingredient in building good models.

Like in the previous examples, let's define some utility functions to take a look at how the model performs against some of the images in the test set:

```
def plot_image_and_predictions(prediction, classes, true_
label, img):
    import numpy as np
    import matplotlib.pyplot as plt

    plt.grid(False)
    plt.xticks([])
    plt.yticks([])
    plt.imshow(np.squeeze(img))
```

```python
    predicted_label = int(np.argmax(prediction))
    confidence = 100 * np.max(prediction)
    color = 'blue' if predicted_label == true_label else 'red'

    plt.xlabel('{predicted} {confidence:2.0f}% ({expected})'.
    format(
        predicted=classes[predicted_label],
        confidence=confidence,
        expected=classes[int(true_label)]), color=color)

def plot_value_array(prediction, true_label):
    import numpy as np
    import matplotlib.pyplot as plt

    plt.grid(False)
    plt.xticks([])
    plt.yticks([])
    thisplot = plt.bar(range(len(prediction)), prediction,
    color="#777777")
    plt.ylim([0, 1])
    predicted_label = np.argmax(prediction)

    thisplot[predicted_label].set_color('red')
    thisplot[true_label].set_color('blue')

# Plot the first X test images, their predicted label, and
the true label
# Color correct predictions in blue, incorrect predictions
in red
def plot_results(images, labels, predictions, classes, rows,
cols):
    n_images = rows * cols
    plt.figure(figsize=(2 * 2 * cols, 2 * rows))
```

```
for i in range(n_images):
    plt.subplot(rows, 2 * cols, 2 * i + 1)
    plot_image_and_predictions(
        predictions[i], classes, labels[i], images[i])

    plt.subplot(rows, 2 * cols, 2 * i + 2)
    plot_value_array(predictions[i], labels[i])

plt.show()
```

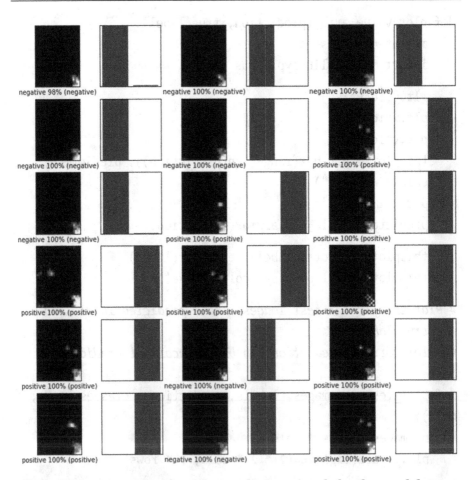

Figure 3-10. *An example of the predictions made by the model over a batch of items of the test set*

And call it with a sample of images from the first test set batch:

```
test_batch = test_data.next()
test_images = test_batch[0]
test_labels = test_batch[1]
predictions = model.predict(test_images)

index_to_label = {
    index: label
    for label, index in train_data.class_indices.items()
}

plot_results(
    images=test_images,
    labels=[np.argmax(label_values) for label_values in
    test_labels],
    classes=index_to_label,
    predictions=predictions,
    rows=6, cols=3)
```

You should see an image like the one shown in Figure 3-10.

3.6 Deploying the model

Once you are happy with the performance of the model, it's time to save it, using a logic similar to the one previously explored to save the label names as well:

```
def model_save(model, target, labels=None, overwrite=True):
    import json
    import pathlib
```

```
# Check if we should save it like a .h5/.pb
# file or as a directory
model_dir = pathlib.Path(target)
if str(target).endswith('.h5') or \
    str(target).endswith('.pb'):
    model_dir = model_dir.parent

# Create the model directory if it doesn't exist
pathlib.Path(model_dir).mkdir(parents=True, exist_
ok=True)

# Save the TensorFlow model using the save method
model.save(target, overwrite=overwrite)

# Save the label names of your model in a separate JSON
file
if labels:
    labels_file = os.path.join(model_dir, 'labels.json')
    with open(labels_file, 'w') as f:
        f.write(json.dumps(list(labels)))

model_dir = os.path.expanduser('~/models/people_detect')

model_save(model, model_dir,
    labels=train_data.class_indices.keys(), overwrite=True)
```

In the preceding snippet, we have saved the model as a TensorFlow model directory (~/models/people_detect), but you can also choose to save it as a single Protobuf (.pb extension) or Hierarchical Data Format (HDF4/HDF5, .h4/.h5 extension) file. Recent versions of TensorFlow can load and save any of these formats, as well as the TensorFlow plugin provided by Platypush does, but if you are planning to import the model into other applications, it's usually a good idea to double-check which formats they support. In any of these cases, the model_save method will also generate a labels.json file if a list of labels is provided—that can help map back the output nodes to the actual human-readable class labels, and I haven't yet found a standard way to natively add them to a TensorFlow model.

Once the model is saved, you are ready to export it to the Raspberry Pi. Go back to the Raspberry Pi and copy it over SSH:

```
mkdir -p ~/models
scp -r user@your-pc:/home/user/models/people_detect ~/models
```

The model files should have now been copied on your Raspberry Pi under /home/pi/models/people_detect. Once the model has been uploaded to the device, we need a way to use it for predictions on live data. There are mainly two ways to use TensorFlow/Keras models on the Raspberry Pi:

1. Use the native **TensorFlow** library.

2. Use **OpenCV**.

Getting both the libraries installed and properly working on Raspberry Pi used to be a little of a technical challenge until some time ago, but if you are using a Raspberry Pi 4 with the most recent version of Raspbian/Raspberry Pi OS (or any other recent supported distribution), it should be relatively easy.

3.6.1 The OpenCV way

Using OpenCV to make predictions from trained models on a Raspberry Pi used to be my favorite solution until some time ago (indeed, I wrote an article back in 2019 that showed how to use a previously trained TensorFlow model to make live predictions on a Raspberry Pi using this approach). However, that was mainly because getting TensorFlow to build and run on a Raspberry Pi used to be a long and tedious process, but things have quite changed on the Raspberry Pi 4. There are mainly two limitations with the OpenCV approach:

1. At the time of writing, the `cv2.dnn` OpenCV package can only read models—it can't be used for live training nor it can save models.

2. The compatibility with TensorFlow formats is quite limited. It can't read models saved in HDF5 format (which need to be converted to Protobuf before being loaded; there are few scripts on the Web to do it), and I have also experienced issues with loading some models saved by recent TensorFlow/Keras versions as well.

However, if your Raspberry Pi architecture/distribution doesn't natively support TensorFlow, OpenCV may be a good alternative to make predictions.

First, you'll have to make sure that OpenCV is installed on the device with the `contrib` package—which is the one that actually contains the `cv2.dnn` module. If you use Raspbian Buster on a Raspberry Pi 4 or more recent versions, this should hopefully be as simple as

```
[sudo] pip3 install opencv-contrib-python
```

If everything went well, check if you can successfully import the module:

```
>>> import cv2.dnn
>>>
```

If anything goes wrong in the process or if you use another OS/
Raspberry Pi/SoC device, look up online for ways to get OpenCV Python3
(and the contrib package) installed on your platform—some users have
posted step-by-step solutions for the most tricky cases.

Once the dependency is in place, you may have to export the HDF5
model to a single Protobuf file—I have had issues importing the directory-
based saved_model.pb models generated by recent TensorFlow versions,
but exporting an .h5 file to .pb still works. There are several tools for this
purpose, for example:

```
git clone https://github.com/amir-abdi/keras_to_tensorflow
cd keras_to_tensorflow
python3 keras_to_tensorflow.py \
    --input_model=/home/pi/models/people_detect/model.h5 \
    --output_model=/home/pi/models/people_detect/exported_
    model.pb
```

Then, using your model for predictions should be as simple as running
these lines:

```
import os
import json
import sys

import numpy as np
import cv2

assert len(sys.argv) >= 2, f'Usage: {sys.argv[0]} <image_
file>'
```

```python
image_file = os.path.expanduser(sys.argv[1])
model_dir = os.path.expanduser('~/models/people_detect')
model_file = os.path.join(model_dir, 'exported_model.pb')
labels_file = os.path.join(model_dir, 'labels.json')

model = cv2.dnn.readNet(model_file)
with open(labels_file, 'r') as f:
    labels = json.load(f)

img = cv2.imread(image_file)
model.setInput(img)
output = model.forward()
class_ = int(np.argmax(output))
label = labels[class_]

print('Predicted label for {img}: {label}. Confidence:
{conf}%'.format(
        img=image_file, label=label, conf=100 * output[class_]))
```

If the preceding script works well, you can use your saved model through the Platypush ml.cv plugin, which exports for free the model over an HTTP API (or any other backend enabled on Platypush, e.g., MQTT, WebSockets, Kafka, etc.). The full interface of the ml.cv is reported on the official documentation. For instance, you can use it to make predictions over cURL (note that the image file must exist on the Raspberry Pi storage):

```
curl -XPOST -u 'user:pass' -H 'Content-Type: application/
json' -d '
{
    "type":"request",
    "action":"ml.cv.predict",
    "args": {
```

```
        "img": "~/dataset/people_detect/positive/
        some_image.jpg",
        "model_file": "~/models/people_detect/
        exported_model.pb",
        "classes": ["negative", "positive"]
    }
}' http://raspberrypi-pi-ip:8008/execute
```

Response:

```
{
  "id": "<response-id>",
  "type": "response",
  "target": "http",
  "origin": "raspberrypi",
  "response": {
    "output": "positive",
    "errors": []
  }
}
```

However, note that the OpenCV Platypush plugin is limited to single images as input and, because of the limitations of the cv2.dnn module, it can only be used for predictions on existing trained models—no live training.

3.6.2 The TensorFlow way

If your device and distribution supports an easy way to install and run TensorFlow, then this may be your favorite way. On a Raspberry Pi 4 with Raspbian Buster or later, this should be possible with these commands:

```
[sudo] apt-get install python3-numpy
[sudo] apt-get install libatlas-base-dev
[sudo] apt-get install libblas-dev
[sudo] apt-get install liblapack-dev
[sudo] apt-get install python3-dev
[sudo] apt-get install gfortran
[sudo] apt-get install python3-setuptools
[sudo] apt-get install python3-scipy
[sudo] apt-get install python3-h5py
[sudo] pip3 install tensorflow keras
```

If it all went fine, you can test if you can run predictions on the previously trained model using the model_load TensorFlow function we saw earlier:

```
import os
import json
import sys

import numpy as np
from tensorflow.keras.models import load_model
from tensorflow.keras.preprocessing import image

assert len(sys.argv) >= 2, f'Usage: {sys.argv[0]} <image_
file>'
image_file = os.path.expanduser(sys.argv[1])
model_dir = os.path.expanduser('~/models/people_detect')
model_file = os.path.join(model_dir, 'saved_model.h5')
labels_file = os.path.join(model_dir, 'labels.json')
```

```python
with open(labels_file, 'r') as f:
    labels = json.load(f)

model = load_model(model_file)

img = image.load_img(image_file, color_mode='grayscale')
data = image.img_to_array(img)

# Remove the extra color dimension if it's a grayscale image
data = np.squeeze(data)

output = model.predict(np.array([data]))[0]
class_ = np.argmax(output)
label = labels[class_]
print('Predicted label for {img}: {label}. Confidence:
{conf}%'.format(
        img=image_file, label=label, conf=100 * output[class_]))
```

If predictions work, you can proceed with testing the model in Platypush to make like predictions through the tensorflow plugin:

```
curl -XPOST -u 'user:pass' -H 'Content-Type: application/
json' -d '
{
    "type":"request",
    "action":"tensorflow.predict",
    "args": {
        "inputs": "~/datasets/people_detect/positive/some_
        image.jpg",
        "model": "~/models/people_detect/saved_model.h5"
    }
}' http://raspberrypi-pi-ip:8008/execute
```

Expected output:

```
{
  "id": "<response-id>",
  "type": "response",
  "target": "http",
  "origin": "raspberrypi",
  "response": {
    "output": {
      "model": "~/models/people_detect/saved_model.h5",
      "outputs": [
        {
          "negative": 0,
          "positive": 1
        }
      ],
      "predictions": [
        "positive"
      ]
    },
    "errors": []
  }
}
```

In this case, outputs contains the values of the output units (with their associated labels if available) for each of the input samples (in this case, we only used one image), and predictions contains either the list of predicted labels for each of the input samples or their class index if labels are not available.

Figure 3-11. *A screenshot of the* `light.hue` *tab in the Platypush web panel*

3.7 Building your automation flows

Now that you are able to use pre-trained models on a Raspberry Pi to make predictions, it's time to leverage Platypush to integrate these predictions into automation flows and run actions on other devices depending on the output of a prediction.

For example, let's build an automation that does the following:

1. It captures pictures at regular intervals (e.g., once a minute) from the thermal camera and stores the captured frame to a temporary JPEG file.

2. If presence is detected, turn on the lights. If presence is not detected, turn off the lights.

We can again leverage Platypush's crons to do this job. I'll cover in this example an implementation with Philips Hue or any smart bulbs compatible with the `light.hue` plugin, but any other device compatible with a Platypush plugin that implements the abstract light plugin should work. First, if you use Philips Hue, then install the Platypush plugin dependencies (it should only include phue):

```
[sudo] pip3 install 'platypush[hue]'
```

And add the following configuration to your config.yaml:

```
light.hue:
    bridge: 192.168.1.123
    groups:
        # Default light groups to be managed
        - Living Room
```

Then restart Platypush and open http://raspberry-pi-ip:8008 in your browser. You may have to authorize the first connection to the Hue bridge by pressing the physical sync button. After the Raspberry Pi has been authorized, refresh the page and you should see a panel like the one shown in Figure 3-11—under the light bulb icon. You can test the connection by trying to switch some lights on or off or change colors. Like all plugins, the actions of light.hue are also available over API, and you can easily embed them in your flows.

For this purpose, we'll create a Platypush procedure as a Python script—it's also possible to do it directly in the config.yaml through the documented YAML syntax, but the YAML syntax is a bit rigid and verbose for complex flows. First, prepare the Platypush user scripts directory if it's not already there:

```
mkdir -p ~/.config/platypush/scripts
touch ~/.config/platypush/scripts/__init__.py
touch ~/.config/platypush/scripts/camera.py
```

You can also add the code of your procedure directly in the __init__.py, but for better modularity, I prefer to group procedures together in modules. Add the following content to camera.py:

```python
import os

from platypush.context import get_plugin
from platypush.procedure import procedure

@procedure
def check_presence(**context):
    # Get plugins by name
    camera = get_plugin('camera.ir.mlx90640')
    tensorflow = get_plugin('tensorflow')
    lights = get_plugin('light.hue')

    image_file = '/tmp/frame.jpg'
    model_file = os.path.expanduser('~/models/people_detect/
    saved_model.h5')

    camera.capture_image(
        image_file=image_file, grayscale=True)

    prediction = tensorflow.predict(
        inputs=image_file, model=model_file)['predictions'][0]

    if prediction == 'positive':
        lights.on()
    else:
        lights.off()
```

Then import the procedure into /.config/platypush/scripts/__
init__.py in order to use it in config.yaml:

```
from scripts.camera import check_presence
```

Finally, replace the previous cron in config.yaml that would simply
capture photos with a new one that calls the newly created procedure
every minute to check for presence:

```
cron.CheckPresenceCron:
    cron_expression: '* * * * *'
    actions:
        - action: procedure.check_presence
```

Restart Platypush, and this should be it—the state of the lights will
change when someone enters or exits the view of the thermal camera.
Time to show off your friends! And remember that Platypush comes with
many other integrations as well—from music, media, and cameras to
cloud services, to many other IoT devices, to MQTT, to voice assistants,
and so on—so you can easily apply the same basic ingredients to build
other smart flows based on live machine learning predictions.

3.8 Building a small home surveillance system

A second example application for a model that can detect the presence
of people is the setup of a small home surveillance system that notifies if
anybody is at home while we are not at home. We can use the following
building blocks to set up such a project:

1. Use an app on your phone that supports geo-fencing—that is, detects when you enter or exit an area—and can trigger actions when such events occur. For this example, we'll be using *Tasker* and *AutoLocation* for Android.

2. Send a message from your phone to the Raspberry Pi, for example, over MQTT when you enter or exit your home area and configure Platypush to listen for such messages and update the HOME state.

3. Keep taking pictures from the thermal camera every minute or so and use the previously trained model to make predictions on the presence of people.

4. If presence is detected and the HOME state is false, then take a picture from an optical camera (e.g., a PiCamera) and send a message back to the phone (e.g., over Pushbullet or Telegram) with the attachment to notify a possible intrusion.

Going step by step, first set up an MQTT server that is accessible both inside and outside of your network. There are several options to achieve this:

1. If you have a Linux box somewhere in the cloud (like an Amazon instance or a VPS), install an MQTT broker like Mosquitto on it—if the box has a public IP address, then it can be accessed by your phone also when it is outside of your home network.

2. If your home network router/provider supports it, use a service like Dyn (formerly DynDNS) to get a hostname for your home router (e.g., my-home-router.gotdns.org) and run a client like ddclient or inadyn to keep the hostname-IP association up to date. Install Mosquitto on your Raspberry Pi or another device in the network and use port forwarding on the router to expose the MQTT port. Note: If you follow this route, you'll basically be exposing a service inside of your network to the outside world. In this scenario, it's advised to set up authentication and encryption on the MQTT server.

3. You can set up a home VPN with, for example, an OpenVPN or WireGuard setup and connect your phone to the same VPN through an Android client. If you run an MQTT broker inside of your home network, it will also be accessible from your phone over the VPN address.

4. Use a public MQTT broker service (like HiveMQ, Adafruit.IO, or MaQiaTTo)—it removes the need for a local installation of Mosquitto, VPNs, and port forwarding, but you may have to pay a bit for a service without limitations.

Whichever option you prefer, at the end of the process, you should have the address and port of an MQTT broker that can be accessed both within and outside of your network. Back to your Raspberry Pi, install the dependencies for the MQTT integration:

```
[sudo] pip3 install 'platypush[mqtt]'
```

Then add the configuration for `backend.mqtt` in your `config.yaml`:

```
backend.mqtt:
    host: your-mqtt-address
    port: 1883
    listeners:
        - topics:
            - sensors/platypush/at_home
```

The `listeners` section instructs Platypush on which topics it should listen for new messages—in this case, we'll be using a topic named sensors/platypush/at_home.

Next, install Tasker and AutoLocation on your (Android) phone. You also need an MQTT client app that supports Tasker integration if you want to send messages from your phone to your MQTT broker—Join, also developed by the same developer that built Tasker and AutoLocation, should be fine if you are using a simple MQTT broker with no authentication or no encryption, but if that's not the case, you should opt for MQTT client. Configure the MQTT app and make sure that it can connect to your broker and receive messages. You can then tune AutoLocation to your preference—for example, whether it should use GPS data, cell ID information, or both; how often it will check the location and configure the background monitor; and so on. Then create a new profile in the Tasker interface that runs on location update. Create a new location centered on your home address and select a sensitivity radius (e.g., 50, 100, or 200 meters). Then create a new task that runs when you enter this area, create a new action, select your MQTT integration, and specify the address and port of your broker, the topic (e.g., sensors/platypush/at_home), and the message (e.g., **1**). Similarly, create a task that runs when you exit the area (long press on the task in the profile and select *Add Exit Task*) and sends **0** to the topic. If it all went well, your phone will start sending *0* or *1* to your MQTT instance on the selected topic whenever you enter or exit your home area.

Platypush triggers a MQTTMessageEvent whenever a new message is received upon a watched topic. You can easily define *hooks* on events, that is, pieces of logic that run whenever an event matching some criteria is received, and they can be created both using the YAML and Python syntax. For example, let's create a hook on the Raspberry Pi that reacts to a new message received on the home presence MQTT topic and sets a state variable that we can use in other scripts or applications to signal whether we are at home or not. Add the following lines to, for example, ~/.config/platypush/scripts/home.py:

```python
from platypush.context import get_plugin
from platypush.event.hook import hook
from platypush.message.event.mqtt import MQTTMessageEvent

@hook(MQTTMessageEvent, topic='sensors/platypush/at_home')
def on_home_state_changed(event, **context):
    # Use the variable plugin to persist state variables
    # on the local storage
    variable = get_plugin('variable')
    variable.set('HOME', int(event.args['msg']))
```

And import the event hook into /.config/platypush/scripts/__init__.py to make it visible to the configuration:

```python
from scripts.home import on_home_state_changed
```

Now the Raspberry Pi will keep the value of the HOME variable in sync whenever you enter or exit the home area.

Next, we'll need some messaging integration to send messages from the Raspberry Pi to your phone when something goes on. There are multiple options to achieve this—send a message over the Pushbullet,

Telegram, or Twilio integrations, send an email, trigger an IFTTT rule, and so on. For the purposes of this example, we'll see how to deliver the message with Pushbullet because it requires the least amount of steps. Install the Pushbullet integration:

```
[sudo] pip3 install 'platypush[pushbullet]'
```

Install the app on your phone as well and head to https://docs. pushbullet.com to get an API access token for your account. Once you have your access token, configure Platypush to use it:

```
pushbullet:
    token: your-token
```

Optionally, if you also want to send a picture of your room at the moment the presence is detected, you'll need an optical camera plugin—camera.pi, camera.ffmpeg, camera.gstreamer, and camera.cv will do the job. For example, if you have a PiCamera, you can install the dependencies:

```
[sudo] pip3 install 'platypush[picamera]'
```

And enable the plugin:

```
camera.pi:
    enabled: True
```

Finally, let's put all the pieces together by modifying the previous check_presence cron so that

1. It captures a picture from the thermal camera.

2. It uses the previously trained model to predict whether someone is in the picture.

3. If we are at home, run the previous logic—turn the lights on if someone is in the picture; turn them off otherwise.

4. If we are not at home and presence is detected, take a picture from the PiCamera and send it to our phone over Pushbullet to notify us that someone may be in our house.

Putting all the pieces together:

```python
import os

from platypush.context import get_plugin
from platypush.procedure import procedure

@procedure
def check_presence(**context):
    # Get plugins by name
    thermal_camera = get_plugin('camera.ir.mlx90640')
    pi_camera = get_plugin('camera.pi')
    variable = get_plugin('variable')
    tensorflow = get_plugin('tensorflow')
    lights = get_plugin('light.hue')
    pushbullet = get_plugin('pushbullet')

    ir_image_file = '/tmp/ir-frame.jpg'
    pi_image_file = '/tmp/pi-frame.jpg'
```

```python
model_file = os.path.expanduser('~/models/people_detect/
saved_model.h5')

# Check if we are at home
response = variable.get('HOME')
at_home = int(response.get('HOME'))

# Capture an image from the thermal camera
thermal_camera.capture_image(
    image_file=ir_image_file, grayscale=True)

# Use the model to predict if there is someone in the picture
prediction = tensorflow.predict(
    inputs=image_file, model=model_file)['predictions'][0]

# If we are at home, run the light on/off logic
if at_home:
    if prediction == 'positive':
        lights.on()
    else:
        lights.off()
elif prediction == 'positive':
    # Otherwise, if presence is detected and we are not
    at home,
    # take a picture from the PiCamera and send it over
    Pushbullet
    # to notify of a possible intrusion
    pi_camera.capture_image(image_file=pi_image_file)
    pushbullet.send_note(body='Possible intrusion
    detected!')
    pushbullet.send_file(filename=pi_image_file)
```

Restart Platypush, and your new home surveillance logic should be in place!

3.9 Live training and semi-supervised learning

A nice feature of having a trained model loaded in memory and with a remote API is that you can train the model in real time with new data and save it, without having to scavenge your laptop for that specific notebook that you used to train it, and with a transparent flow that can be logged on a remote service.

Moreover, this approach can be used to train models incrementally as more data is processed. In the case of Platypush, the tensorflow plugin exposes the tensorflow.train method for live training of loaded models. Example train session over cURL:

```
# Load the model from disk
curl -XPOST -u 'user:pass' -H 'Content-Type: application/
json' -d '
{
    "type":"request",
    "action":"tensorflow.load",
    "args": {
        "model": "~/models/people_detect/saved_model.h5"
    }
}' http://raspberrypi-pi-ip:8008/execute

# Train the model with some new data.
# For instance, a new camera picture that we already
# know to be positive.
curl -XPOST -u 'user:pass' -H 'Content-Type: application/
json' -d '
{
    "type":"request",
```

```
    "action":"tensorflow.train",
    "args": {
        "model": "~/models/people_detect/saved_model.h5",
        "inputs": ["/home/pi/datasets/people_detect/positive/
        some-image.jpg"],
        "outputs": ["positive"]
    }
}' http://raspberrypi-pi-ip:8008/execute

# Save the model once done
curl -XPOST -u 'user:pass' -H 'Content-Type: application/
json' -d '
{
    "type":"request",
    "action":"tensorflow.save",
    "args": {
        "model": "~/models/people_detect/saved_model.h5"
    }
}' http://raspberrypi-pi-ip:8008/execute

# Unload the model once saved to save memory
curl -XPOST -u 'user:pass' -H 'Content-Type: application/
json' -d '
{
    "type":"request",
    "action":"tensorflow.unload",
    "args": {
        "model": "~/models/people_detect/saved_model.h5"
    }
}' http://raspberrypi-pi-ip:8008/execute
```

The `inputs` field on the `train` API is quite flexible, and it currently supports lists of images, CSV/TSV files, numpy uncompressed/compressed files, and raw arrays, and the API exposes other useful attributes as well—such as batch size, number of epochs, validation data and validation split, weights, and so on.

The live training approach is particularly interesting for an approach I like to call *tutor learning*. You can equip your Raspberry Pi with other devices to get hunches for the presence of people—such as motion detectors, light detectors, or cameras mounted in different points of the room. You can configure a cron that runs data captures on all of these devices at the same time. Once one of the sensors detects presence (e.g., through motion), then the corresponding picture taken from the thermal camera at the same time will be labelled as positive and used to train the model in real time. Similarly, the model can be paired with the output of a luminosity sensor, building inferences such as "if it's dark in the room, and no motion is detected, and the time is between midnight and 8 AM, then it's likely that the pictures taken in this time frame include no people."

As a result, you can build a training logic that is kind of semi-supervised, based on data points from other sensors that can more deterministically track the metric that you want to predict. If you move your newly trained model to another machine or you simply remove the accessory sensors, the model should still be as good as tracking presence as if the other sensors or cameras were still there.

As another example, you can train a model for people detection from optical camera images that uses data from the thermal camera model as a *tutor*. We have explored earlier the reason why a thermal source is more reliable in a small environment than an optical camera to detect the presence of people. However, you can first train a detection model on the basis of the output of a thermal camera and then create a cron that captures frames at the same time both from the thermal sensor and the optical camera. If the accuracy of the thermal model is very high, then its predictions can be used as labels for the optical camera frames and used to feed a real-time dynamic dataset to, for example, a more sophisticated CNN architecture. After performing sufficient live training of the model using this (semi)automated strategy, and once the performance metrics of the model are satisfactory enough, the thermal camera can be unplugged, and the stand-alone optical camera model should still be able to make predictions.

3.10 Classifiers as a service

To conclude the exploration of the possibilities offered by the synergy between TensorFlow models and IoT tools, let's see an example where the whole management of the previous model for people detection over MLX90640 happens over a service (e.g., Platypush) instead of a notebook.

Platypush offers an API to create and compile models, besides training them and using them for predictions—although other popular IoT solutions like Home Assistant may also offer similar features if they provide a TensorFlow integration. The advantage of this approach is that the model will be internally and consistently managed by the service. Moreover, the training logic occurs over API calls or crons/event hooks instead of a (sometimes messy and hard to track) Jupyter notebook.

For example, the MLX90640 presence detection model can be dynamically created via API call:

```
curl -XPOST -u 'user:pass' -H 'Content-Type: application/
json' -d '
{
  "type": "request",
  "action": "tensorflow.create_network",
  "args": {
    "name": "people_detect",
```

```
    "output_names": ["negative", "positive"],
    "optimizer": "adam",
    "loss": "categorical_crossentropy",
    "metrics": ["accuracy"],
    "layers": [
      {
        "type": "Flatten",
        "input_shape": [24, 32]
      },
      {
        "type": "Dense",
        # ~= 0.8 * 32 * 24
        "units": 614,
        "activation": "relu"
      },
      {
        "type": "Dense",
        # ~= 0.3 * 32 * 24
        "units": 230,
        "activation": "relu"
      },
      {
        "type": "Dense",
        "units": 2,
        "activation": "softmax"
      }
    ]
  }
}' http://raspberrypi-pi-ip:8008/execute
```

The `tensorflow.create_network` action does the same as the `keras.Sequential` call we have used earlier to define the model. It can be used to define the model name, the output labels, the optimizer, loss function, performance metrics, and the structure of the network. We can then train the model with our collected data:

```
curl -XPOST -u 'user:pass' -H 'Content-Type: application/
json' -d '
{
  "type": "request",
  "action": "tensorflow.train",
  "args": {
    "model": "people_detect",
    "epochs": 5,
    "inputs": "~/datasets/ir_presence_detector/images",
    "validation_split": 0.3
  }
}' http://raspberrypi-pi-ip:8008/execute
```

We are using our previously defined dataset of camera images organized into the negative and positive sub-folders and specify the number of epochs and the validation split—in this case, 30% of the images will be used for model validation.

The `tensorflow.train` action will generate several events during the training phase that you can attach to if you want to create your custom hooks—for example, copy the model to another machine once the training has completed if the performance metrics haven't degraded, or remove images that belong to batches already processed if you are working on continuous streams, or log the performance of the model over the epochs to a CSV file. Some of these events are

1. `TensorflowTrainStartedEvent`—when the training starts

2. `TensorflowTrainEndedEvent`—when the training phase ends

3. `TensorflowBatchStartedEvent`—when a batch starts being processed

4. `TensorflowBatchEndedEvent`—when a batch is processed

5. `TensorflowEpochStartedEvent`—when a training epoch begins

6. `TensorflowEpochEndedEvent`—when a training epoch ends

At the end of the process, the HTTP client should receive an output that looks like this:

```
{
  "response": {
    "output": {
      "model": "people_detect",
      "epochs": [
        0,
        1,
        2,
        3,
        4
      ],
      "history": {
        "loss": [
          0.9747824668884277,
```

```
            0.6165147423744202,
            0.07518807053565979,
            0.06354894489049911,
            0.06809689849615097
        ],
        "accuracy": [
            0.9494661688804626,
            0.9843416213989258,
            0.9957295656204224,
            0.9950177669525146,
            0.9928825497627258
        ],
        "val_loss": [
            0.5309795141220093,
            0.4760192930698395,
            0.10130093991756439,
            0.32663050293922424,
            0.7078392505645752
        ],
        "val_accuracy": [
            0.9834162592887878,
            0.9850746393203735,
            0.9917080998420715,
            0.9867330193519592,
            0.9834162592887878
        ]
    }
  },
  "errors": []
 }
}
```

Each field of the history reports the loss and performance metric over the training and validation sets for each of the epochs. Once you are happy with the model, you can save it:

```
curl -XPOST -u 'user:pass' -H 'Content-Type: application/
json' -d '
{
    "type":"request",
    "action":"tensorflow.save",
    "args": {
        "model": "people_detect"
    }
}' http://raspberrypi-pi-ip:8008/execute
```

The model will be saved under ~/.local/share/platypush/ tensorflow/models/people_detect. It can be imported into other applications compatible with TensorFlow models or into your own scripts for predictions, and it can easily be reloaded in Platypush on restart:

```
curl -XPOST -u 'user:pass' -H 'Content-Type: application/
json' -d '
{
    "type":"request",
    "action":"tensorflow.load",
    "args": {
        "model": "people_detect"
    }
}' http://raspberrypi-pi-ip:8008/execute
```

And used for real-time predictions:

```
curl -XPOST -u 'user:pass' -H 'Content-Type: application/
json' -d '{
  "type": "request",
  "action": "tensorflow.predict",
  "args": {
    "model": "people_detect",
    "inputs": "/path/to/an/image.jpg"
  }
}' http://raspberrypi-pi-ip:8008/execute
```

This should cover all the steps on how to create, train, evaluate, and manage your models using a remote API—and, ideally, without writing a line of code.

Bibliography

[1] DONALD HEBB. The Organization of Behavior.

[2] ANDREAS KAPLAN, MICHAEL HAENLEIN. *Siri, Siri, in my hand: Who's the fairest in the land? On the interpretations, illustrations, and implications of artificial intelligence* (https://doi.org/10.1016%2Fj.bushor.2018.08.004).

[3] *A Brief History of Computing* (www.alanturing.net/turing_archive/pages/Reference%20Articles/BriefHistofComp.html).

[4] *Raspberry Pi benchmarks* (www.researchgate.net/publication/333973011_Raspberry_Pi_4B_32_Bit_Benchmarks).

[5] *IBM704* (https://en.wikipedia.org/wiki/IBM_704).

[6] H. A. SIMON, ALLEN NEWELL. *Heuristic Problem Solving: The Next Advance in Operations Research* (https://doi.org/10.1287%2Fopre.6.1.1).

[7] H. A. SIMON. *The Shape of Automation for Men and Management.*

[8] M. MINSKY. *Computation: Finite and Infinite Machines.*

[9] M. MINSKY. *Meet Shaky, the First Electronic Person, Life Magazine*, pp. 58–68.

© Fabio Manganiello 2021
F. Manganiello, *Computer Vision with Maker Tech*,
https://doi.org/10.1007/978-1-4842-6821-6

[10] *rmsprop optimizer description* (www.cs.toronto.
edu/~tijmen/csc321/slides/lecture_slides_
lec6.pdf).

[11] S. ZHANG, A.E. CHOROMANSKA, Y. LECUN. *Deep
learning with elastic averaging SGD* (https://
papers.nips.cc/paper/5761-deep-learning-
with-elastic-averaging-sgd.pdf).

[12] D. KINGMA, J. BA. Adam: *A Method for
Stochastic Optimization* (https://arxiv.org/
abs/1412.6980v8).

[13] I. SUTSKEVER, J. MARTENS, G. DAHL, G. HINTON. *On
the importance of initialization and momentum in
deep learning* (www.cs.toronto.edu/~fritz/absps/
momentum.pdf).

[14] *Auto MPG dataset* (https://archive.ics.uci.edu/
ml/datasets/auto+mpg).

[15] *Moore-Penrose inverse* (https://en.wikipedia.
org/wiki/Moore%E2%80%93Penrose_inverse).

[16] JUDITH A HIRSCH, LUIS M MARTINEZ. *Visual Cortical
and Subcortical Receptive Fields* (https://link.
springer.com/referenceworkentry/10.1007%
2F978-3-540-29678-2_6348).

[17] JUDITH A HIRSCH, LUIS M MARTINEZ. *Circuits that
build visual cortical receptive fields* (https://
pubmed.ncbi.nlm.nih.gov/16309753/).

[18] KEVIN R. DUFFY, DAVID H. HUBEL. *Receptive field
properties of neurons in the primary visual cortex
under photopic and scotopic lighting conditions* (www.
ncbi.nlm.nih.gov/pmc/articles/PMC2951600/).

[19] SUMIT SAHA. *A Comprehensive Guide to Convolutional Neural Networks*—the ELI5 way (https://towardsdatascience.com/a-comprehensive-guide-to-convolutional-neural-networks-the-eli5-way-3bd2b1164a53).

[20] IRWIN SOBEL. *An Isotropic 3x3 Image Gradient Operator* (www.researchgate.net/publication/239398674_An_Isotropic_3_3_Image_Gradient_Operator).

[21] F. MOUTARDE, G. DEVINEAU. *Deep-Learning: Introduction to Convolutional Neural Networks* (http://people.mines-paristech.fr/fabien.moutarde/ES_MachineLearning/Practical_deepLearning-convNets/convnet-notebook.html).

[22] *Fruits 360 Kaggle dataset* (www.kaggle.com/moltean/fruits).

[23] *Raspberry Pi home page* (www.raspberrypi.org).

[24] *Pimoroni MLX90640 breakout* (https://shop.pimoroni.com/products/mlx90640-thermal-camera-breakout).

[25] *Breakout Garden* (https://shop.pimoroni.com/products/breakout-garden-hat-i2c-spi).

[26] *NOOBS* (www.raspberrypi.org/downloads/noobs/).

[27] *Raspberry Pi OS* (www.raspberrypi.org/downloads/).

[28] *Platypush Gitlab page* (https://git.platypush.tech/platypush/platypush).

[29] *Platypush modules documentation* (https://platypush.readthedocs.io/en/latest/).

Index

A

Accuracy, 8, 33, 111, 113, 126
Activation function, 90, 91, 93, 94, 101, 153
Artificial intelligence, 2–6, 90
Artificial neural network, 90, 93
AutoLocation, 209, 211
Average pooling, 144, 145

B

Backends, 171, 178
Back-propagation, 6, 96–98, 102

C

categorical_crossentropy loss function, 32, 154
Classification error, 73, 97, 111
Convolutional layer, 135, 136, 137, 142–145
Convolutional neural networks (CNN), 134
  architecture, 135
  convolutional layers, 138, 140, 142, 143
  features, 135
  fully connected/dropout, 145

kernel/filter, 136
pooling layer, 144
recognition, 146–148
training epochs, 155
training set, 150
Cost function, 21, 23, 24, 26, 32, 42, 63, 64, 73, 75, 96–98, 101
Cross-entropy functions, 125, 126

D

Deep learning, 8, 32
Dropout technique, 146

E

Eigenvalue, 48–50
Expert system, 2, 7, 8

F

False negatives (FN), 112, 126
False positives (FP), 112, 115, 184
fit_generator method, 154

G

Grayscale thermal picture, 181

© Fabio Manganiello 2021
F. Manganiello, *Computer Vision with Maker Tech*,
https://doi.org/10.1007/978-1-4842-6821-6

Printed in the United States
By Bookmasters